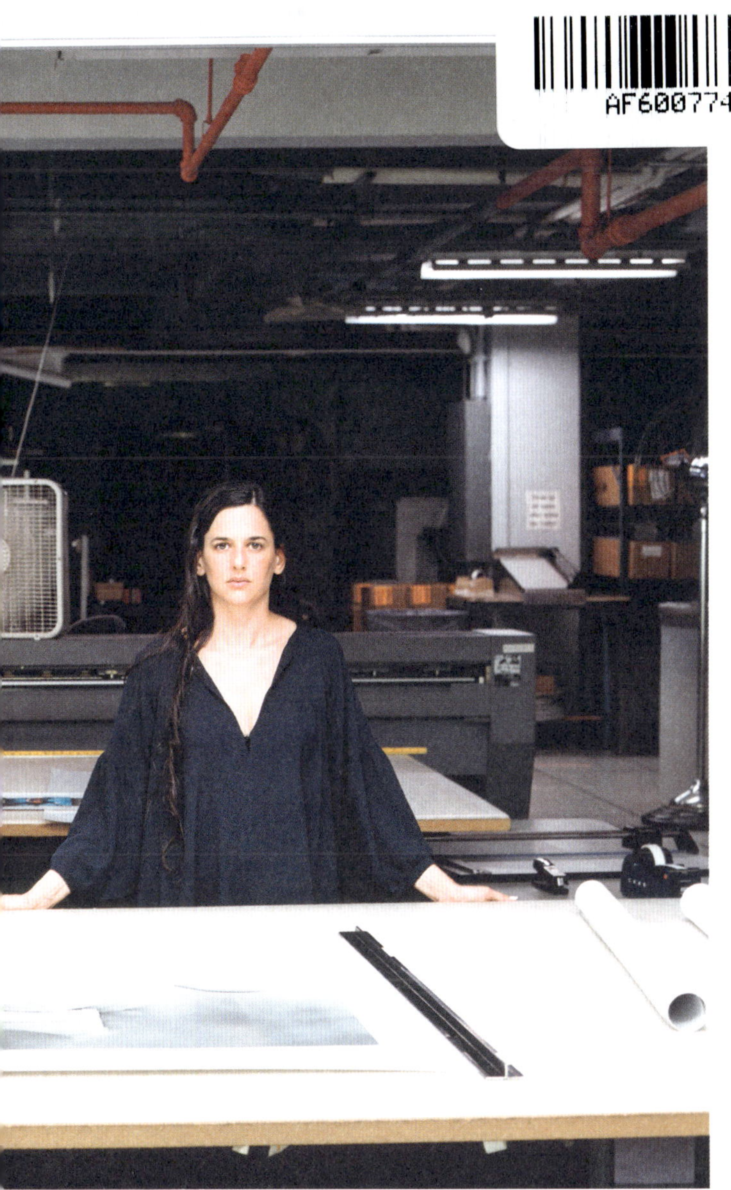

Taryn Simon, Artist, New York City 2007

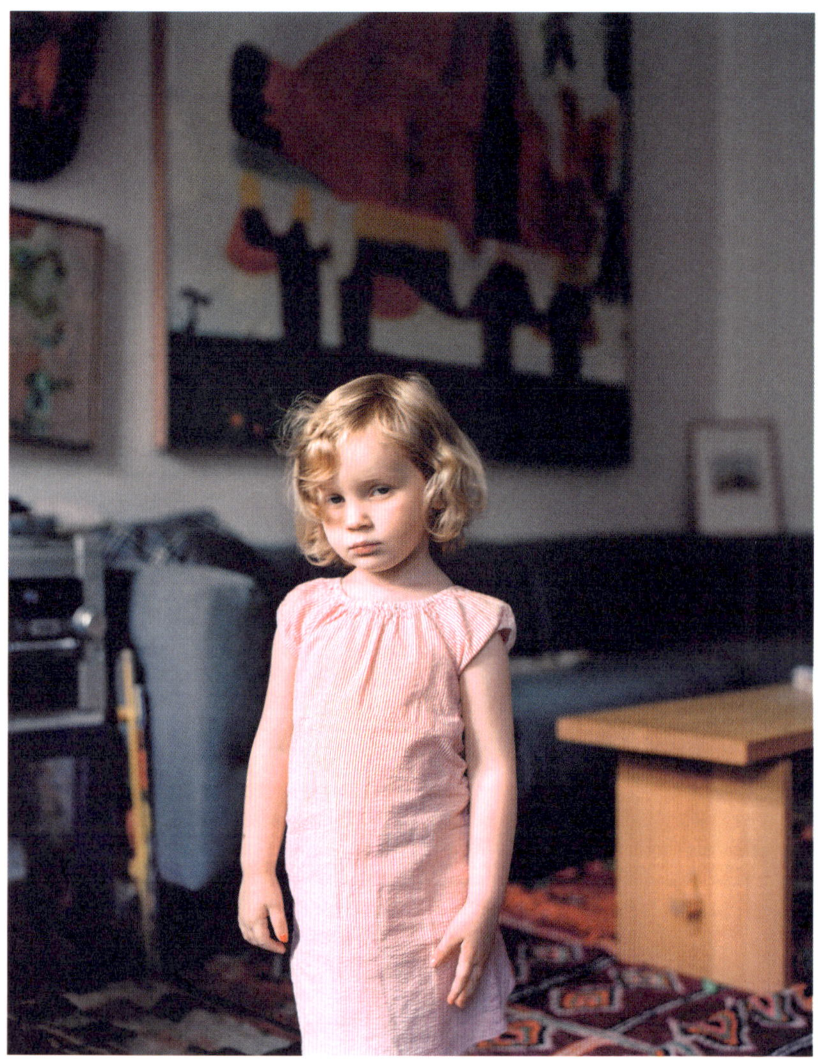

Bella Brunnet, Berlin 2004

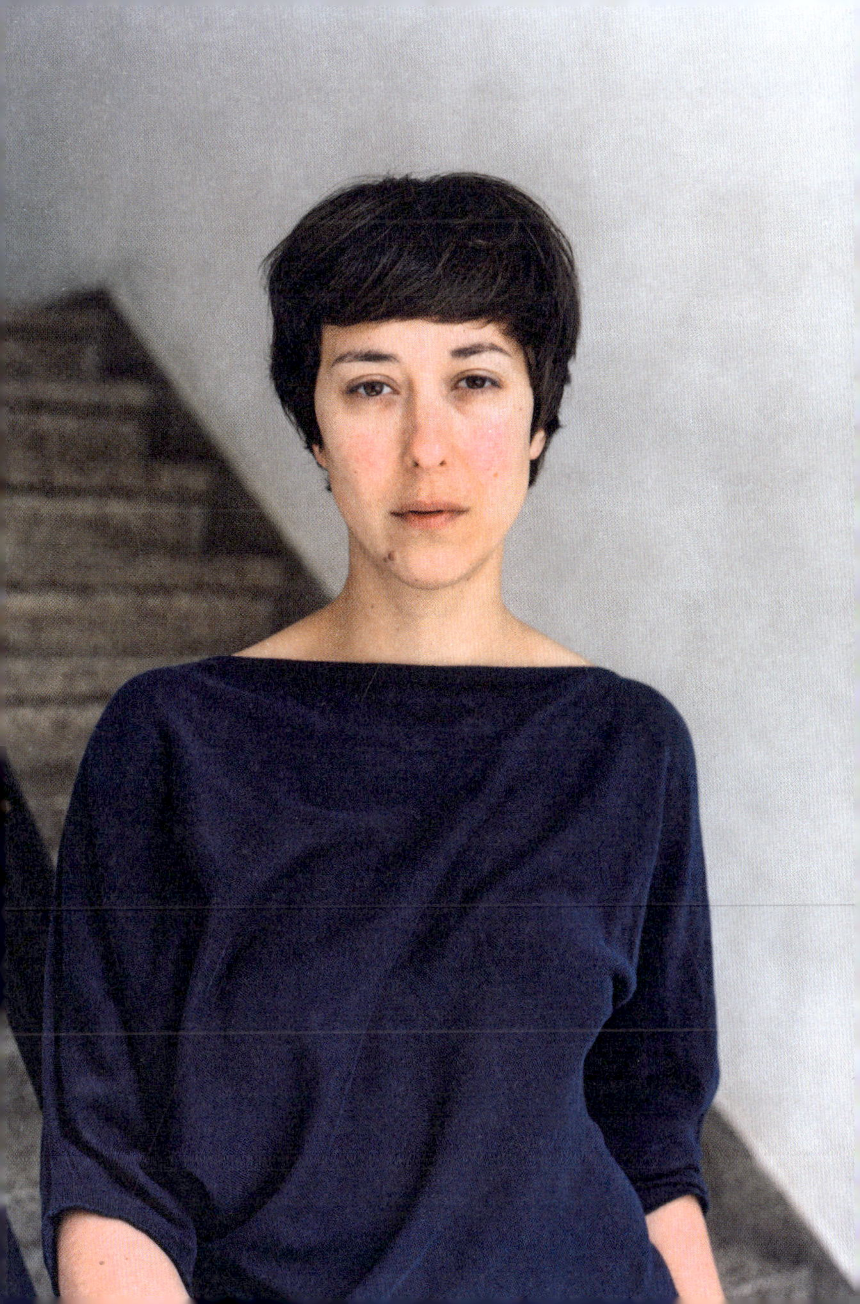

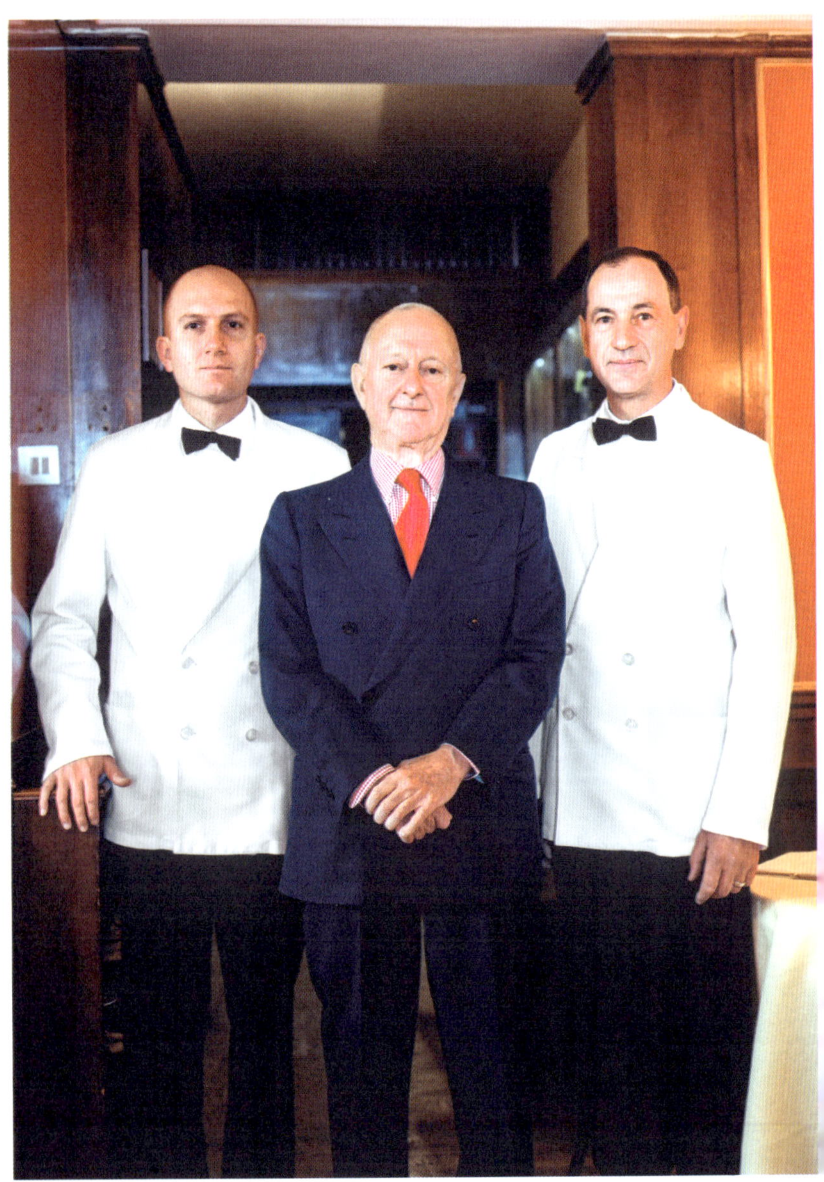

Arrigo Cipriani and collaborators, Harry's Bar, Venezia 2007*
Cover: Marieta Chirulescu, Artist, Berlin 2011

Albrecht Fuchs Fifty-Three Portraits and a Haystack

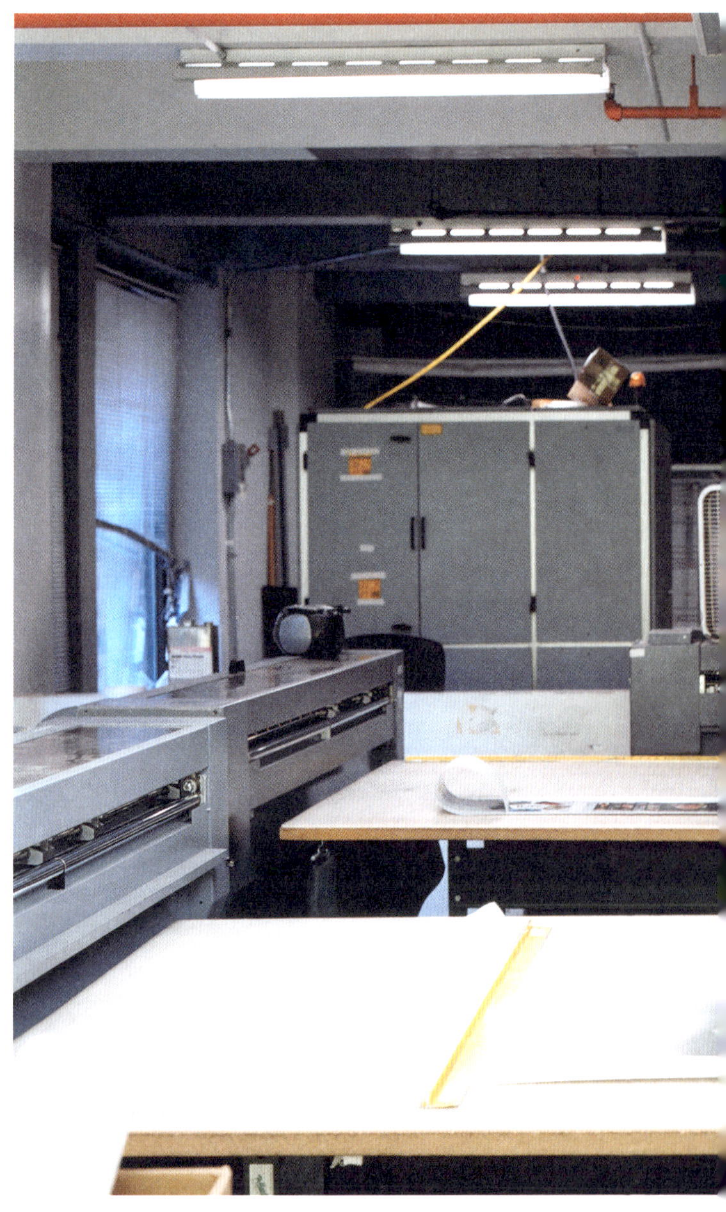

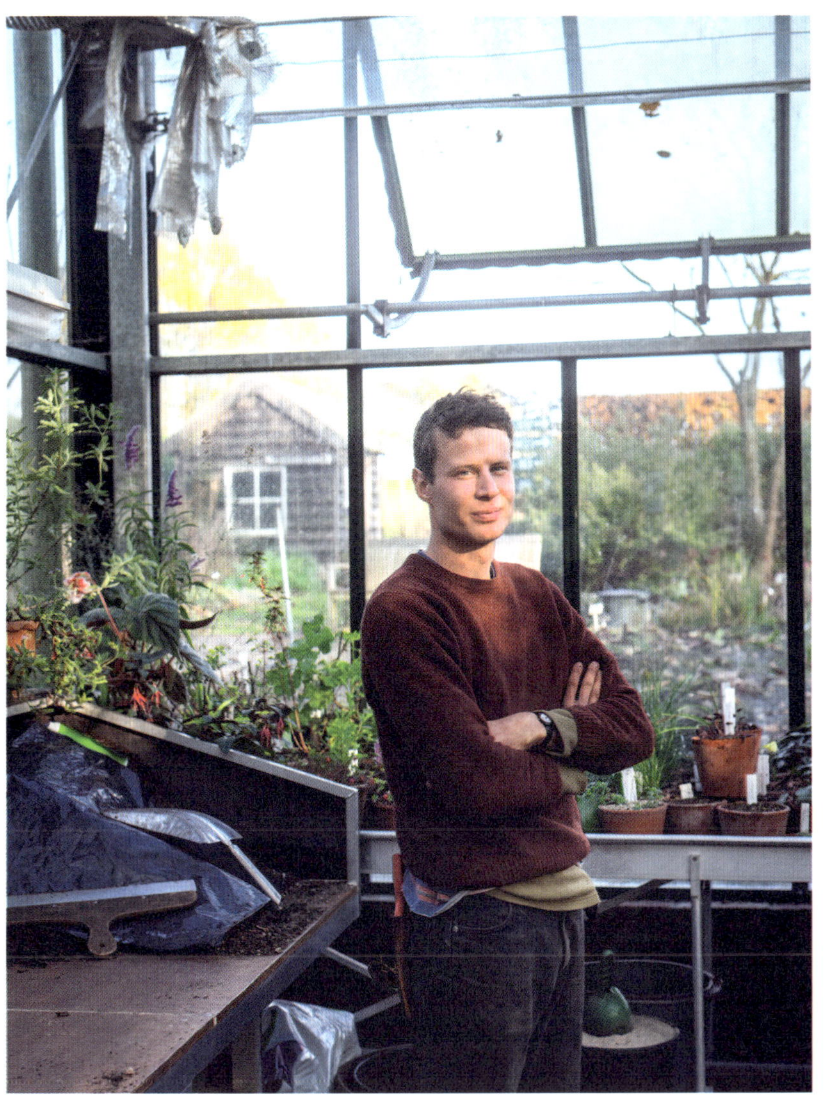

Jonny Bruce, Gardener, Ede/The Netherlands 2017

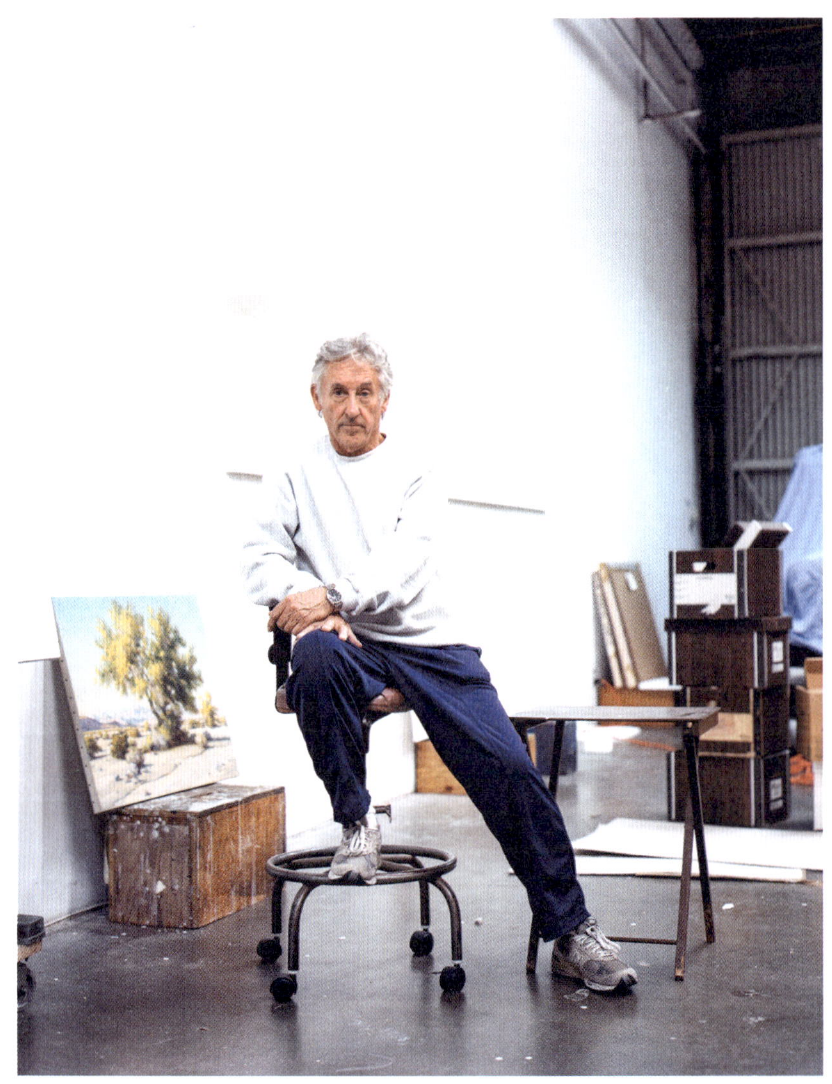

Ed Ruscha, Artist, Los Angeles 2006

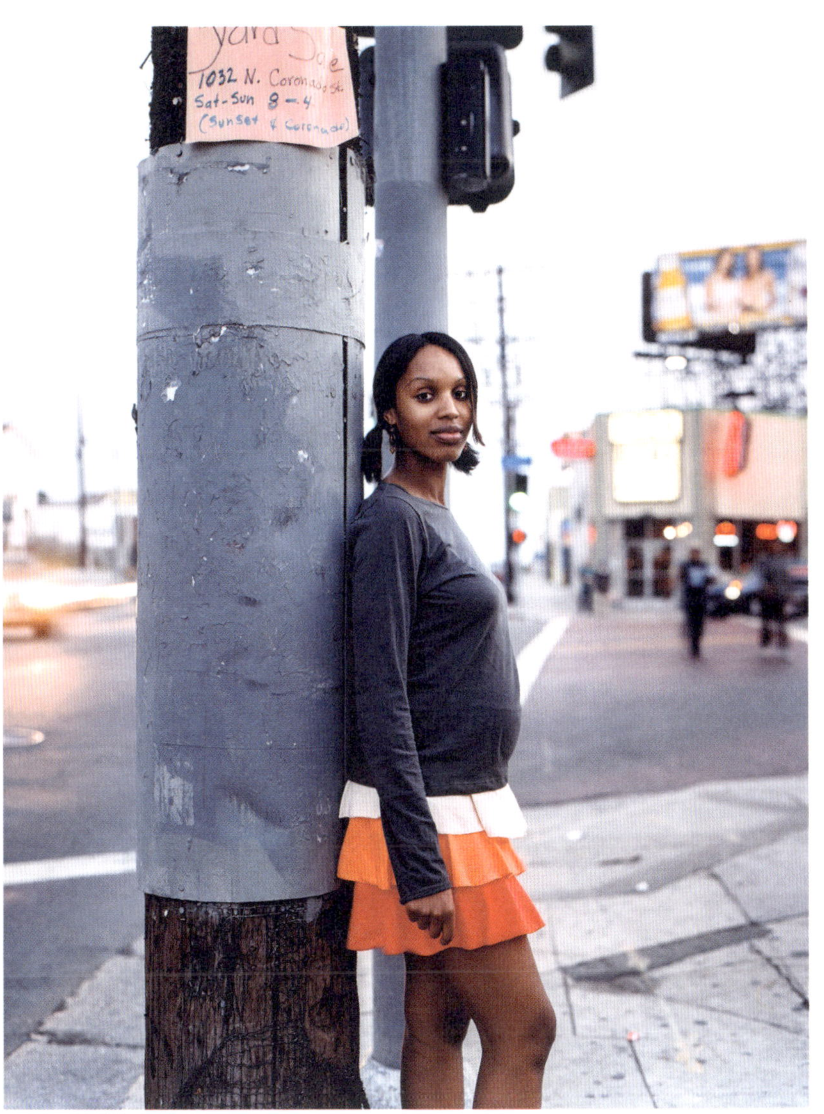

Enisa Banks, Stylist, Los Angeles 2004

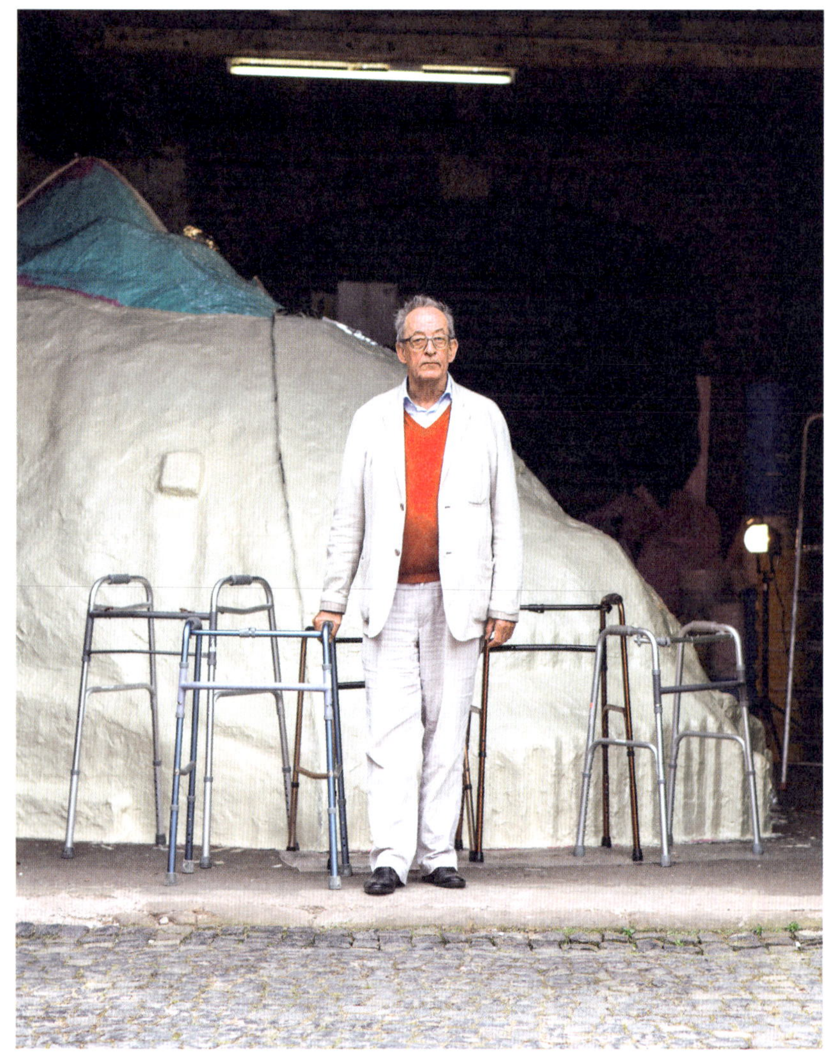

Kaspar König, Curator, Havixbeck 2017

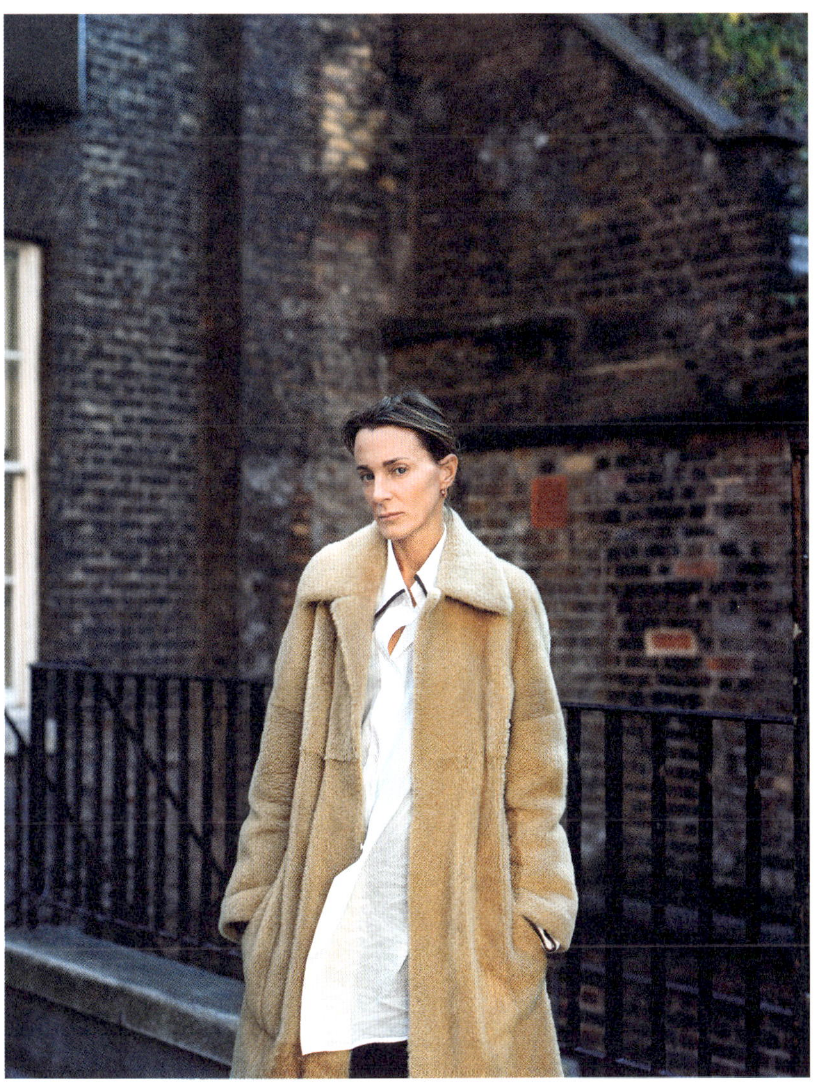

Phoebe Philo, Fashion Designer, London 2016

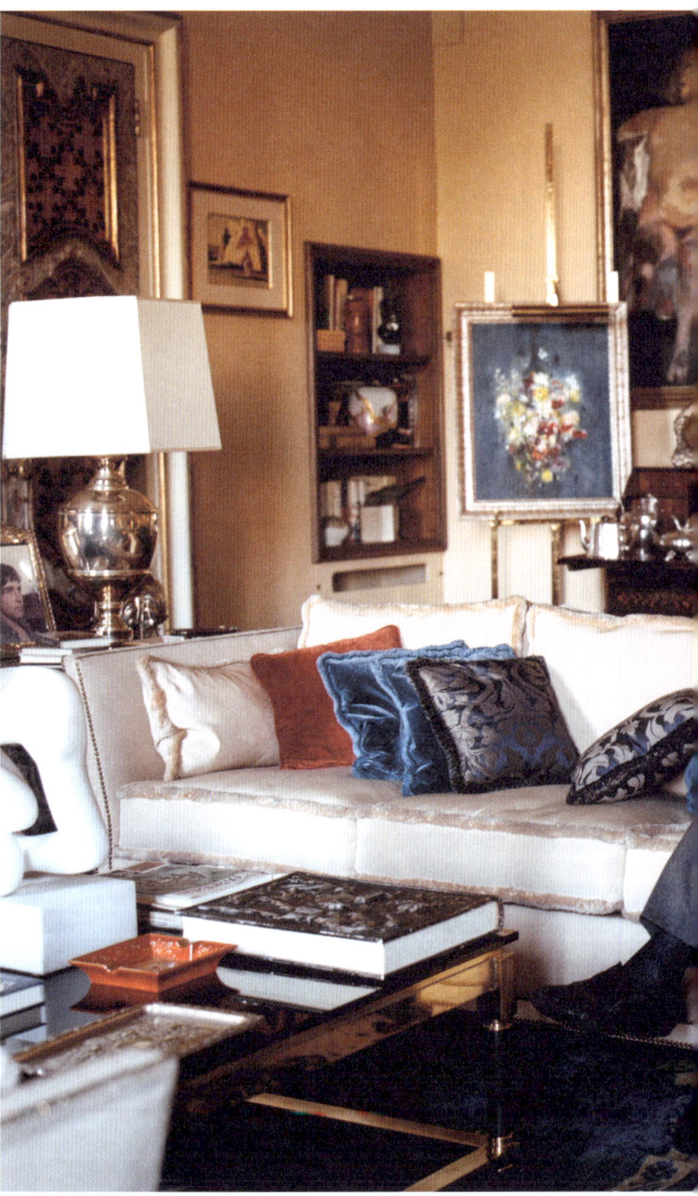

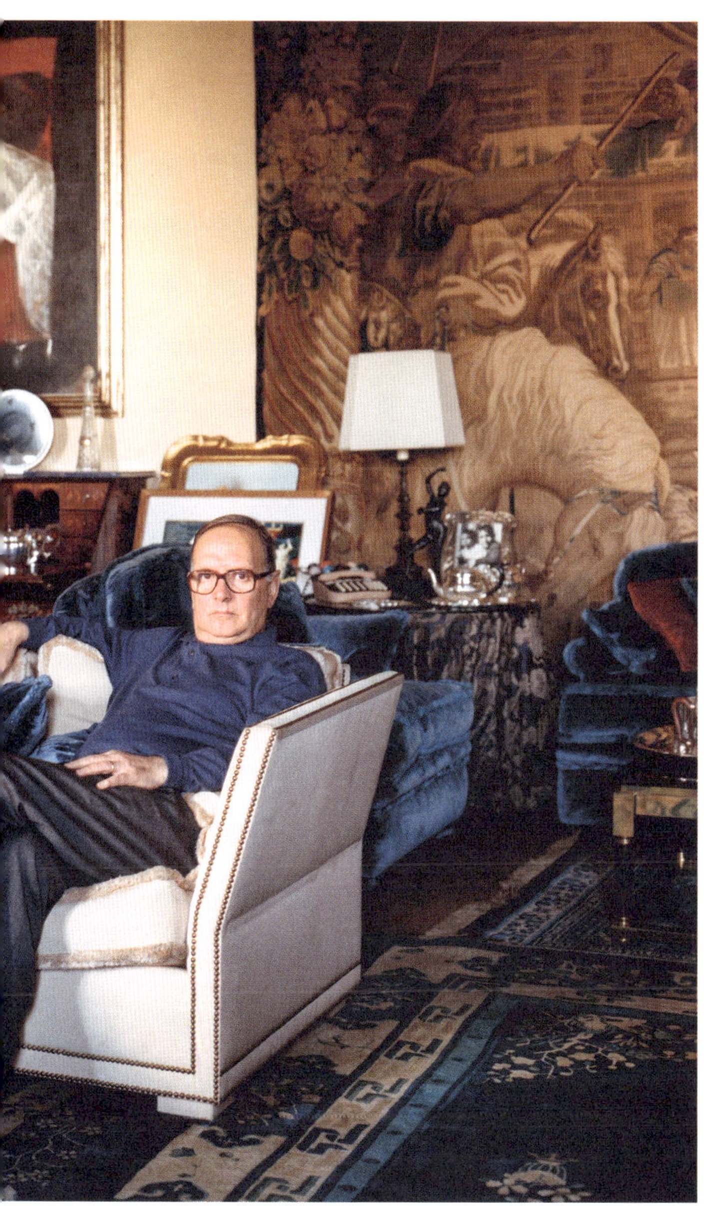

Ennio Morricone, Composer, Rome 1994

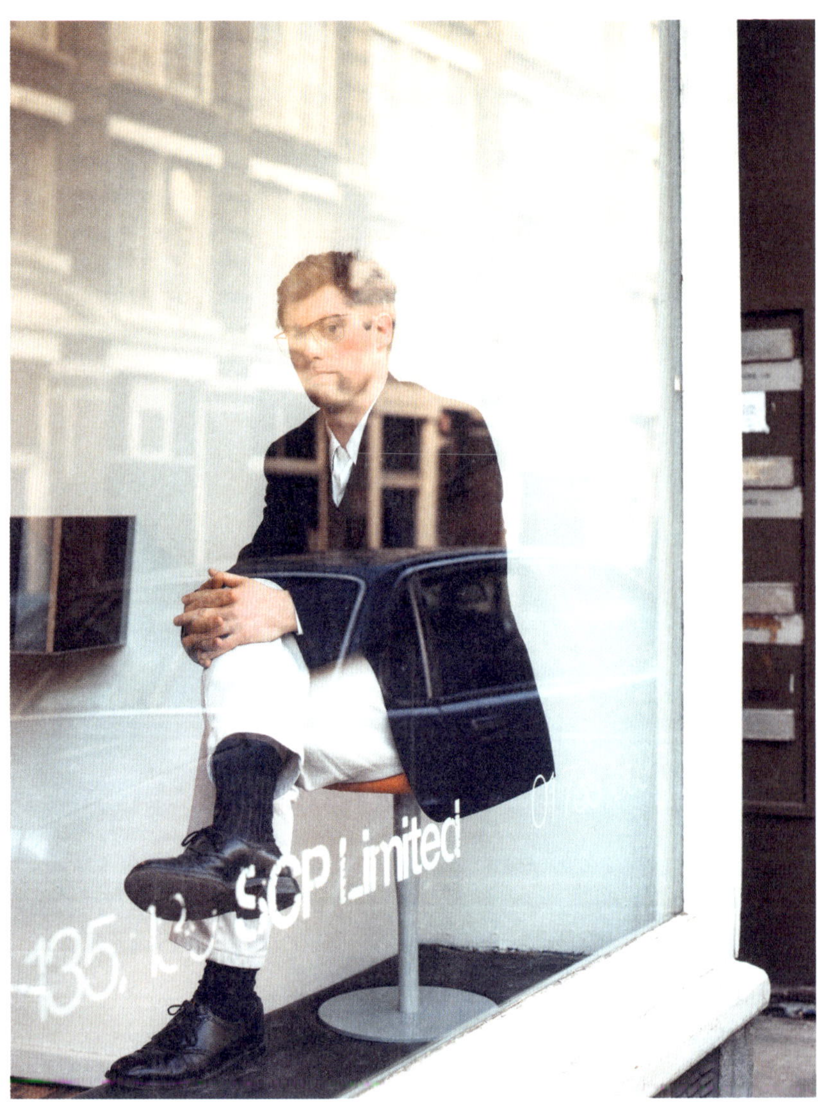

Jasper Morrison, Industrial Designer, London 1994

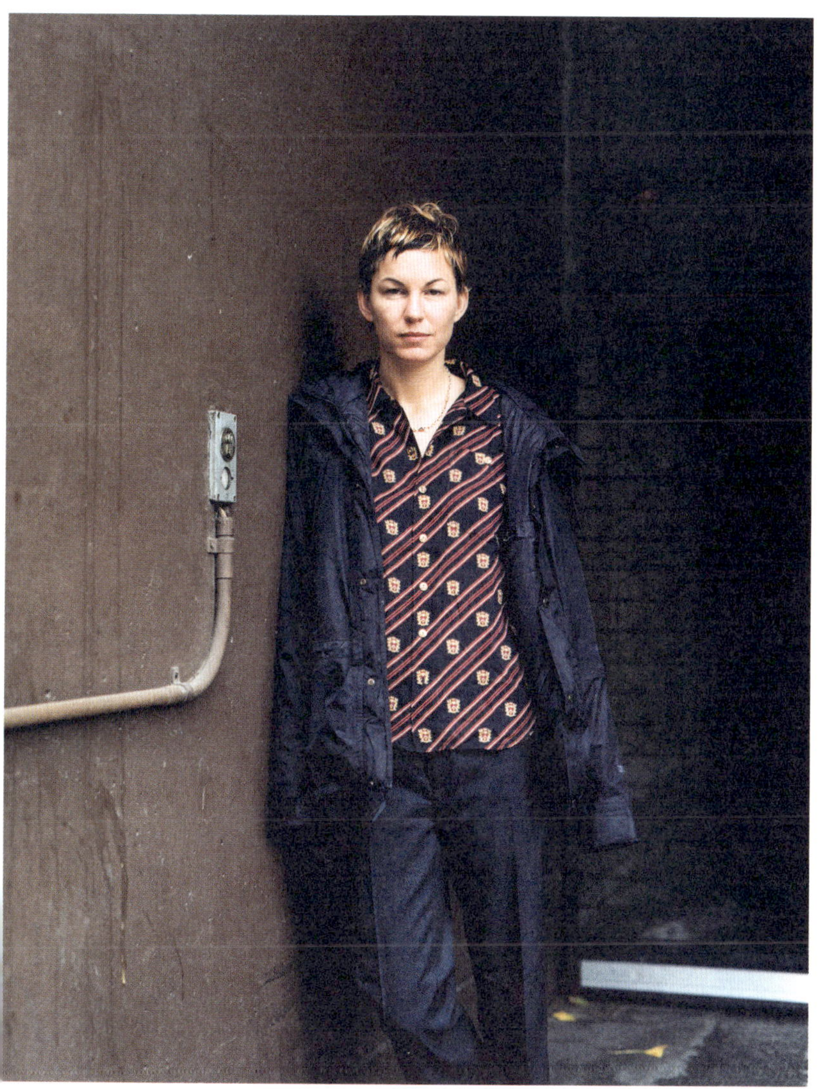

Elizabeth Peyton, Artist, Cologne 1996

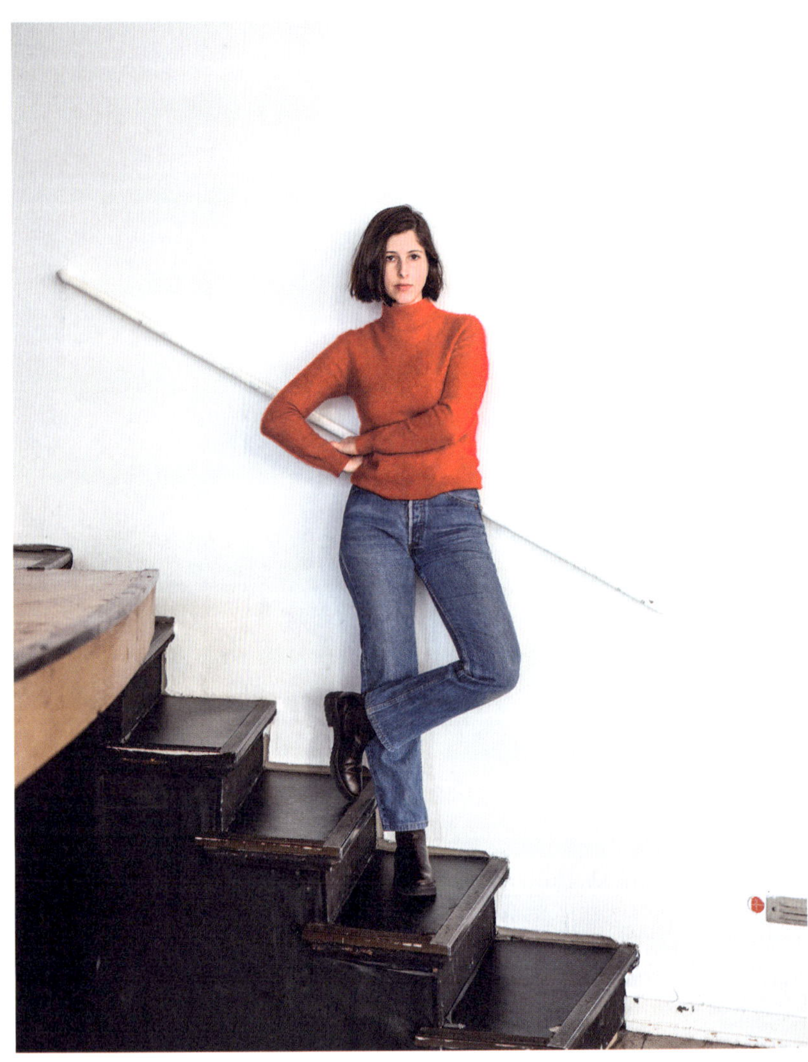

Talia Chetrit, Artist, Cologne 2018

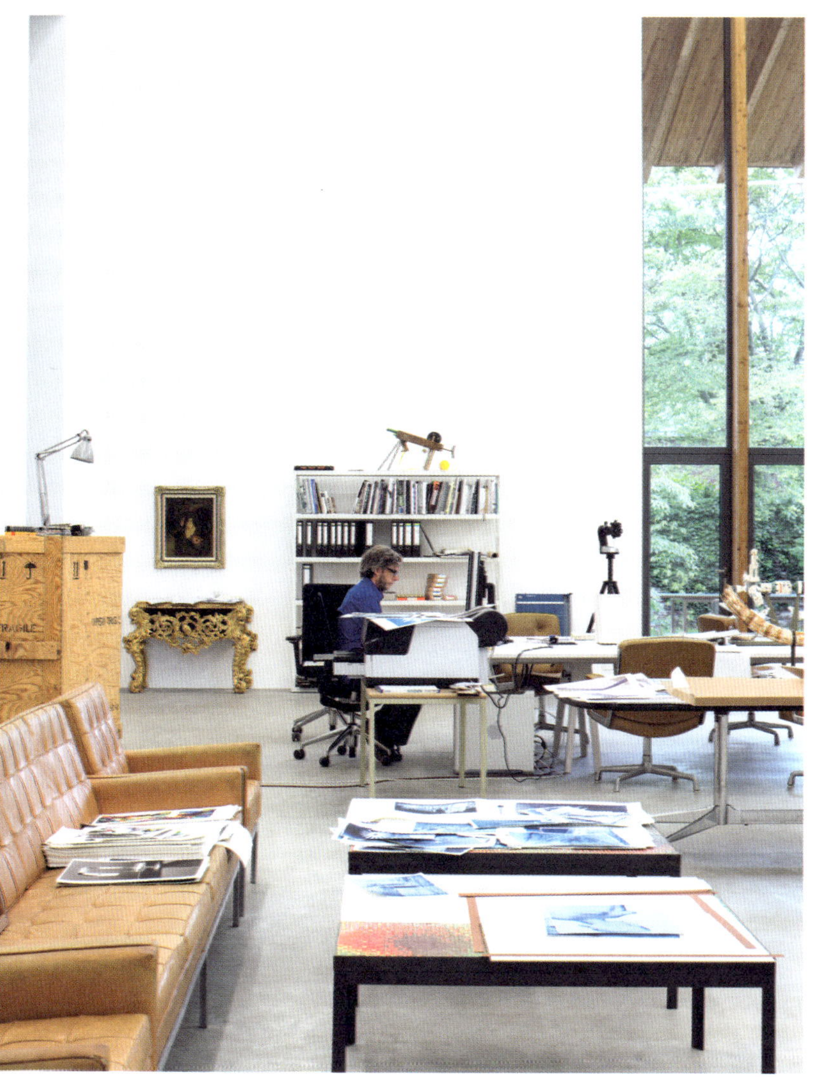

Thomas Ruff, Artist, Düsseldorf 2014

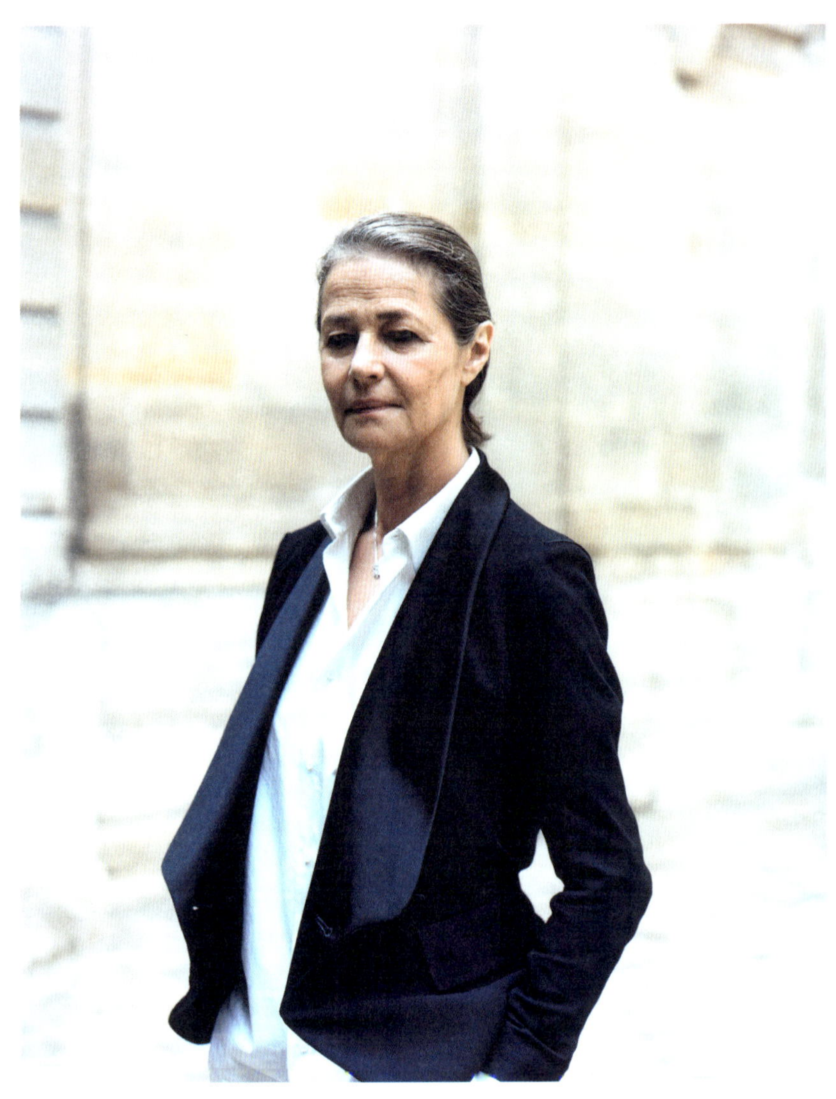

Charlotte Rampling, Actress, Paris 2009

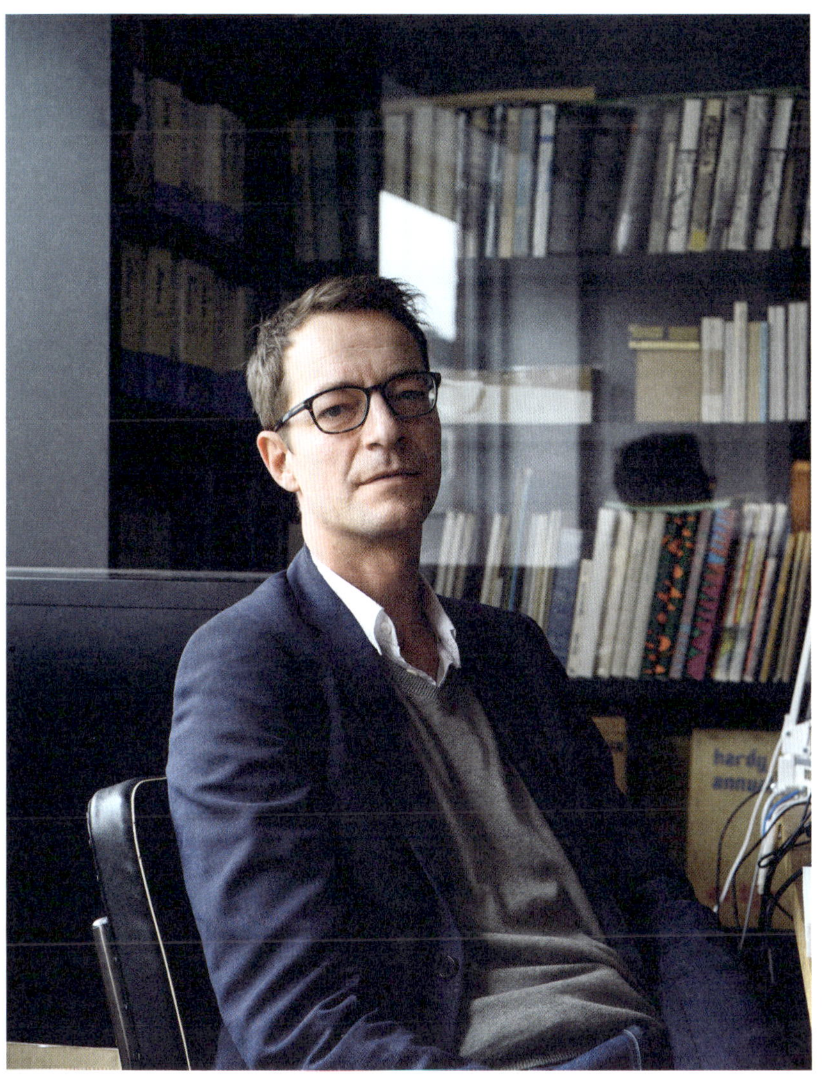

Franz König, Publisher and Bookseller, Cologne 2016

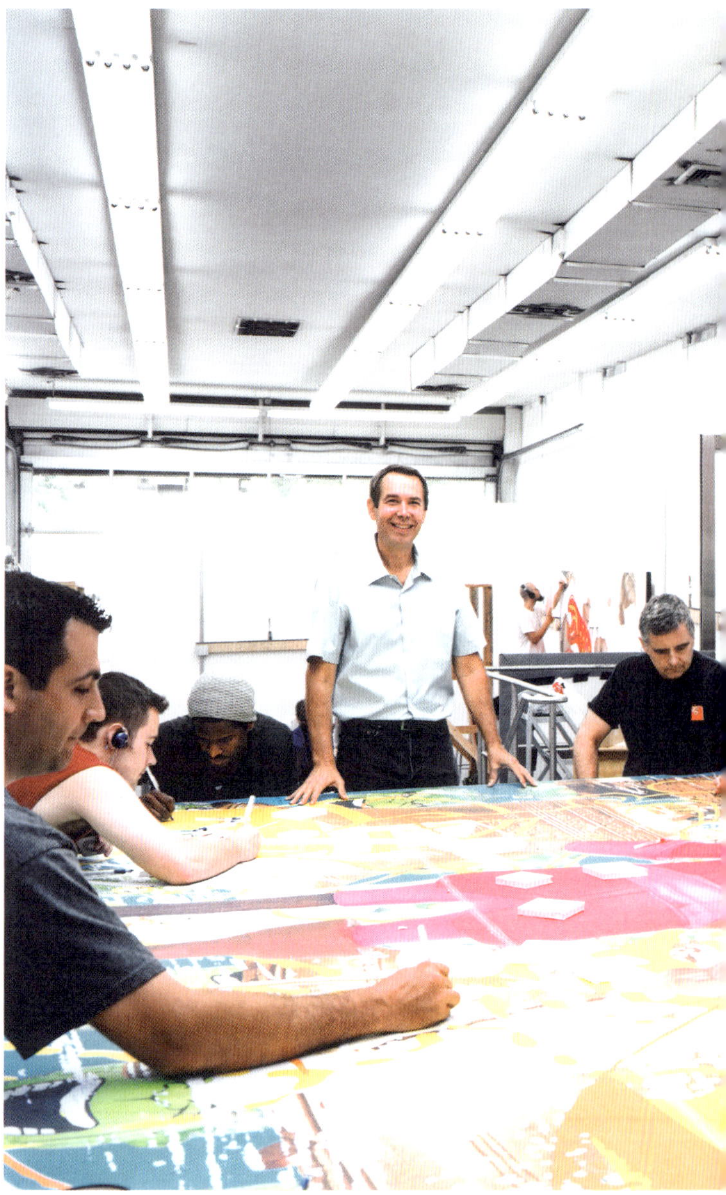

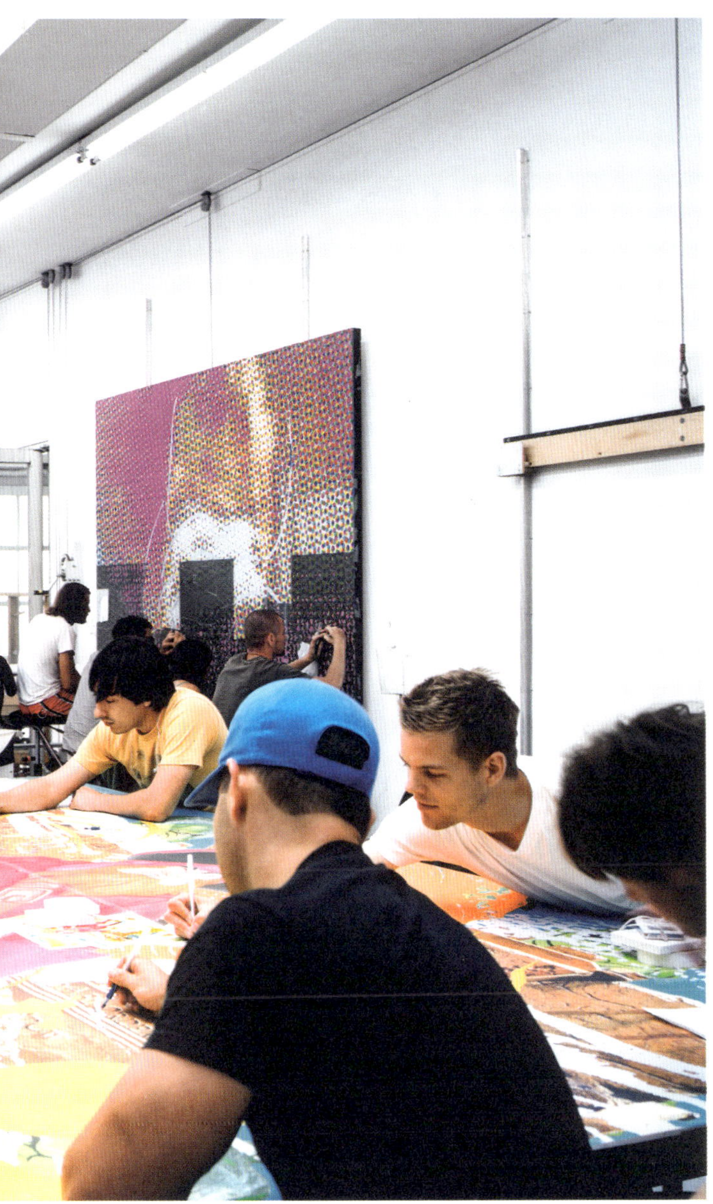

Jeff Koons, Artist, New York City 2007

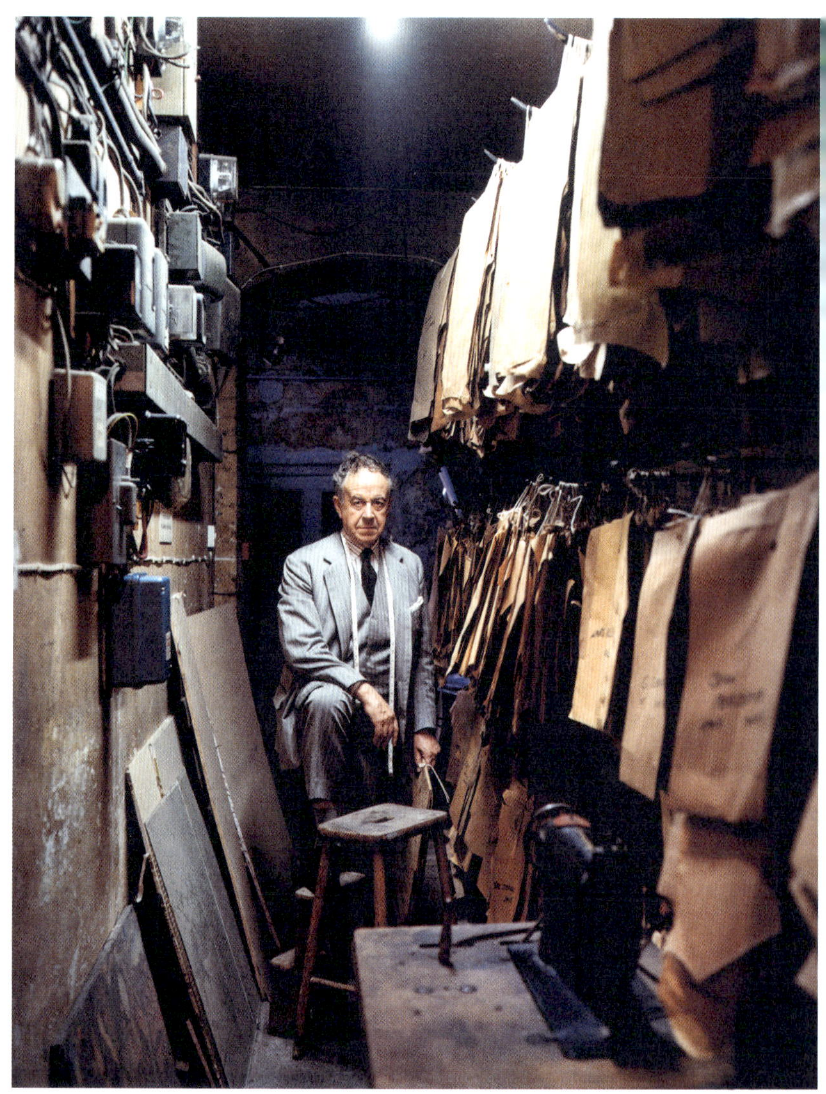

Dennis Wilkinson, Bespoke Taylor, London 1992

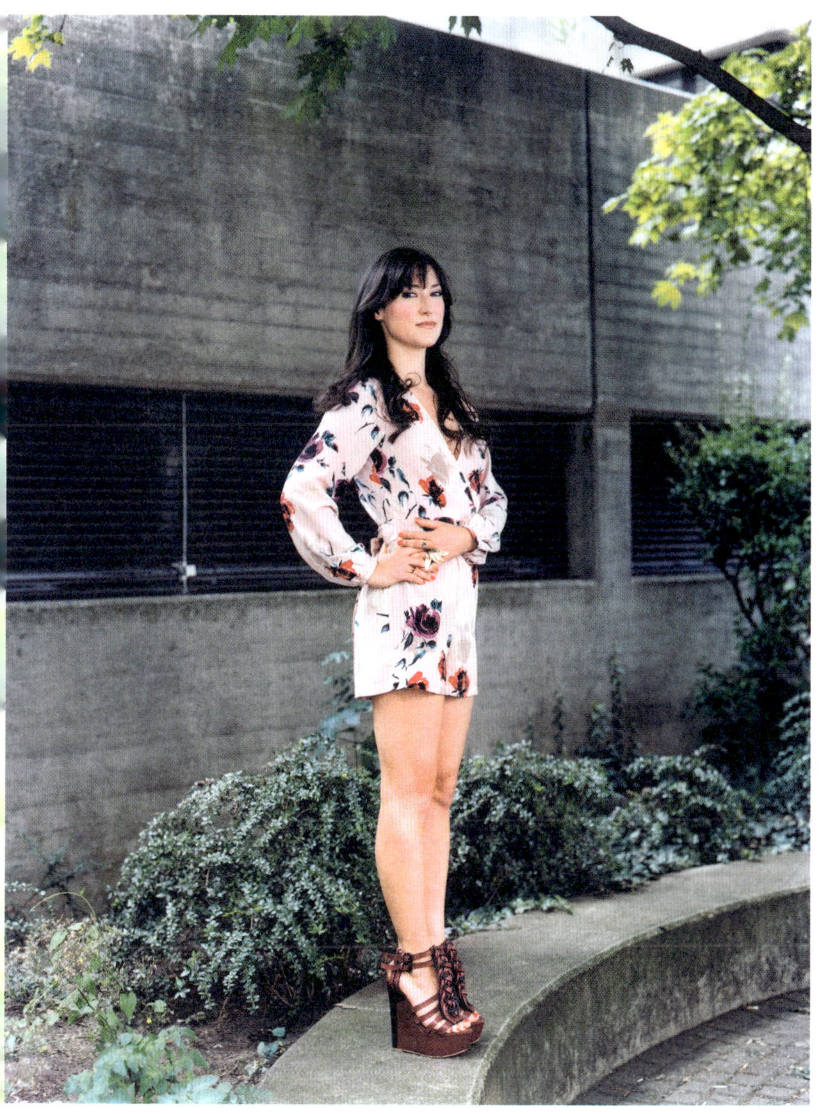

Charlotte Roche, Writer, Cologne 2011

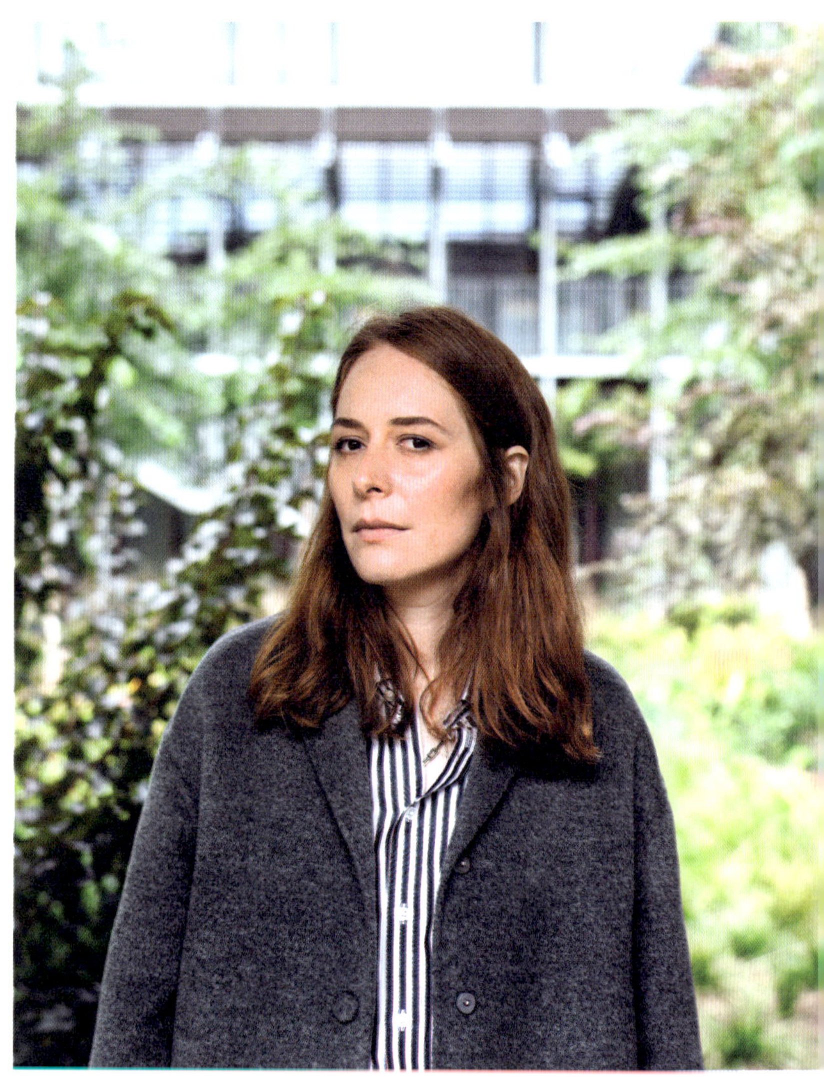

Nadège Vanhee-Cybulski, Fashion Designer, Paris 2015

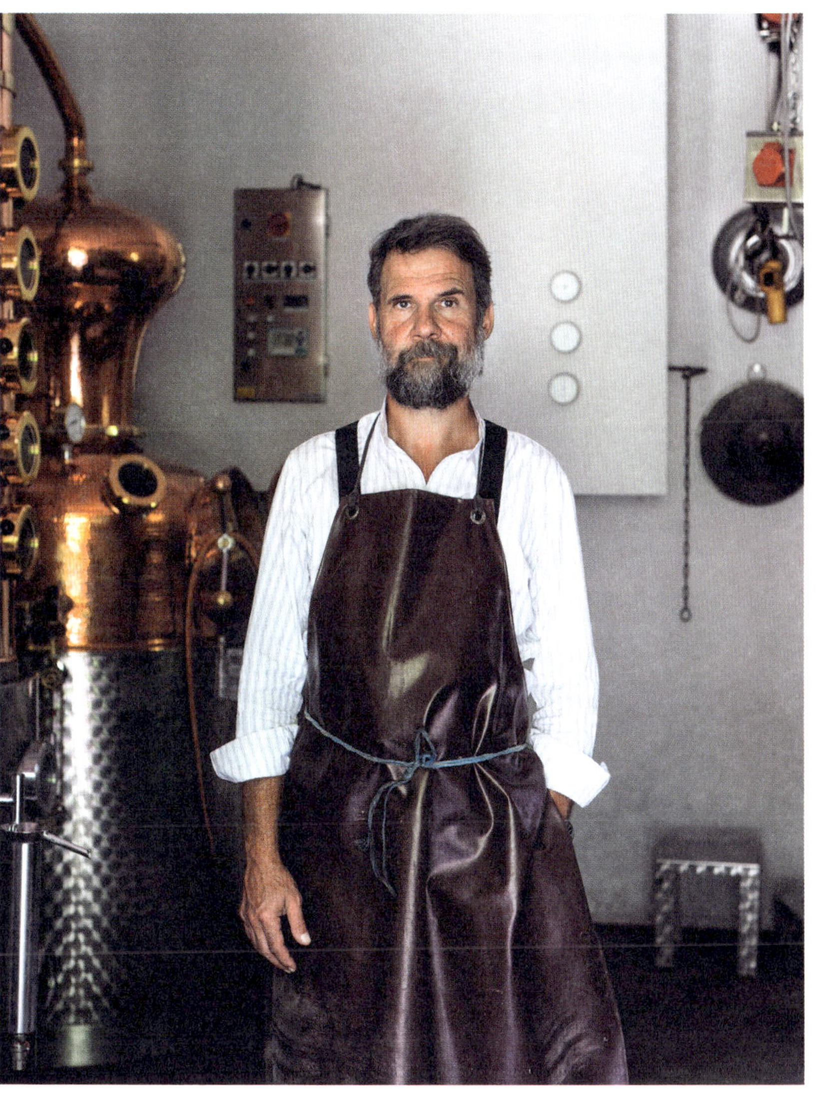

Christoph Keller, Destiller and Publisher, Eigeltingen/Germany 2016

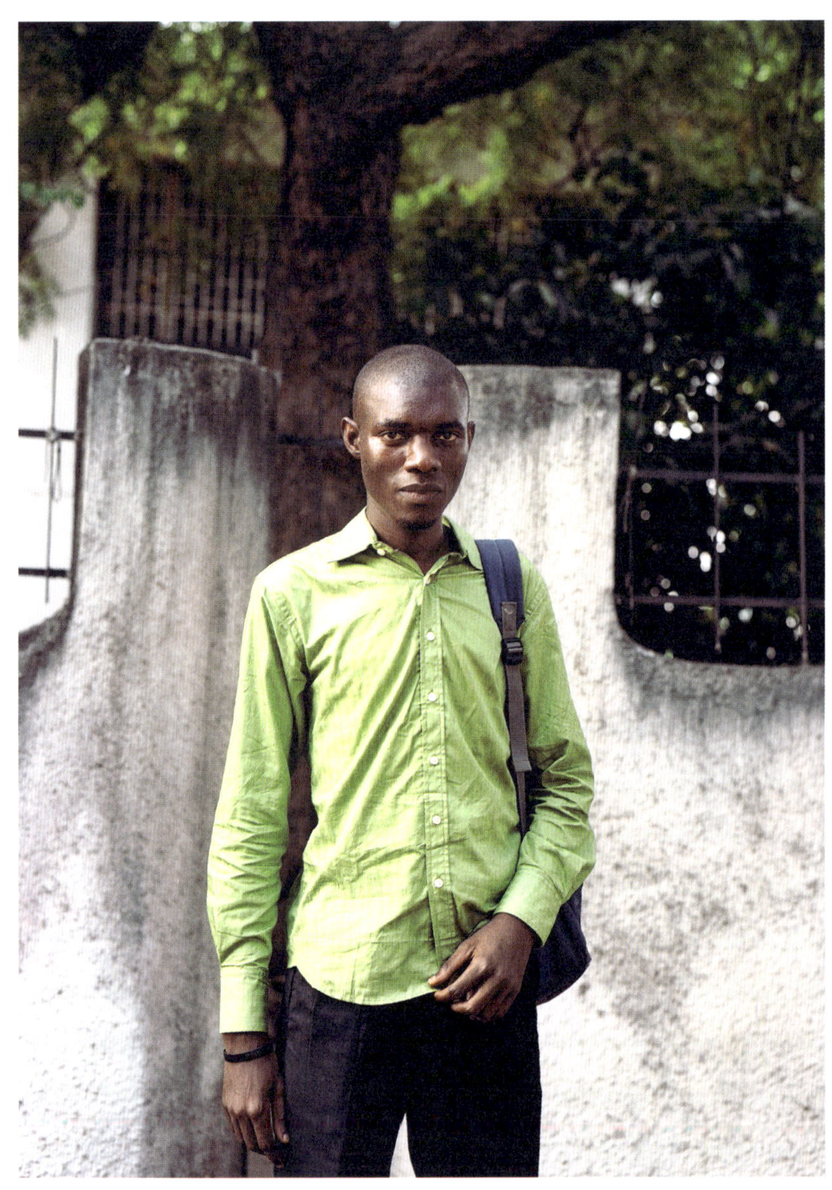

Nentawe Goymar, Student, Lagos/Nigeria 2008

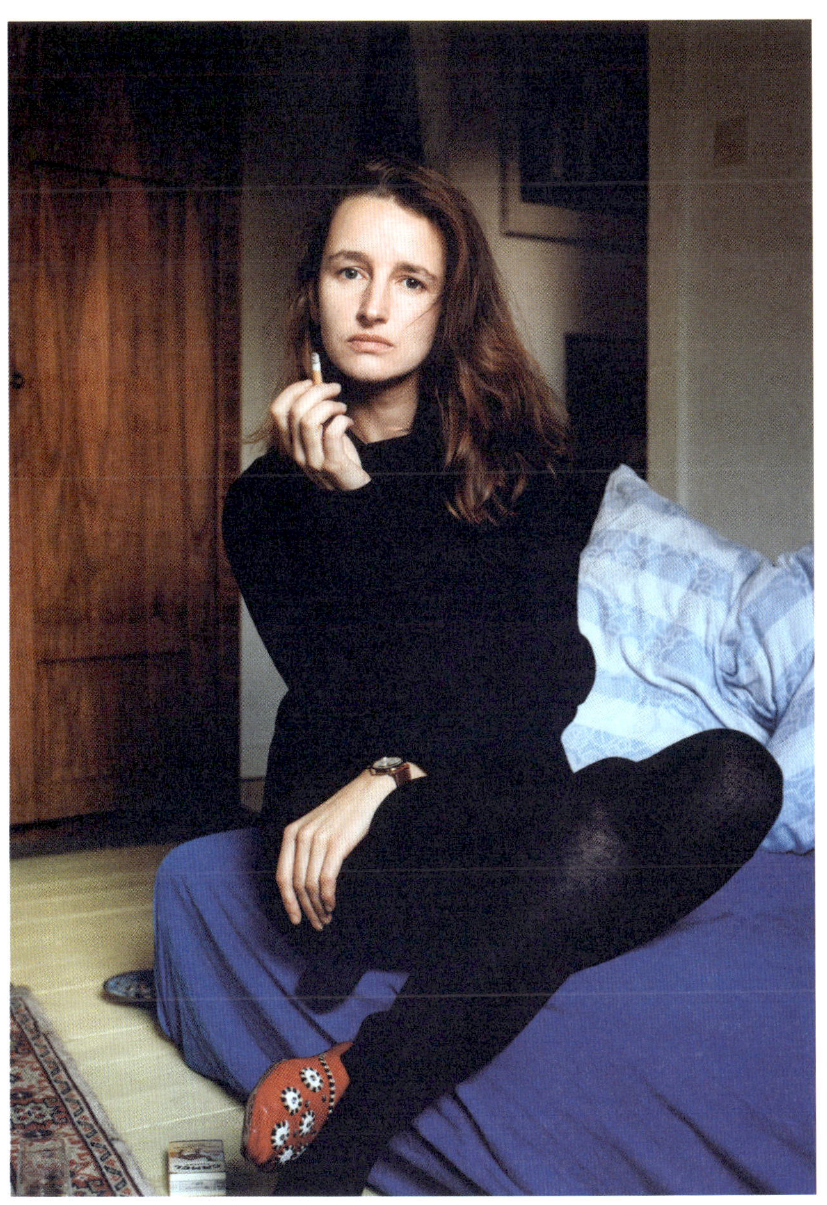

Jitka Hanzlová, Artist, Essen 1991

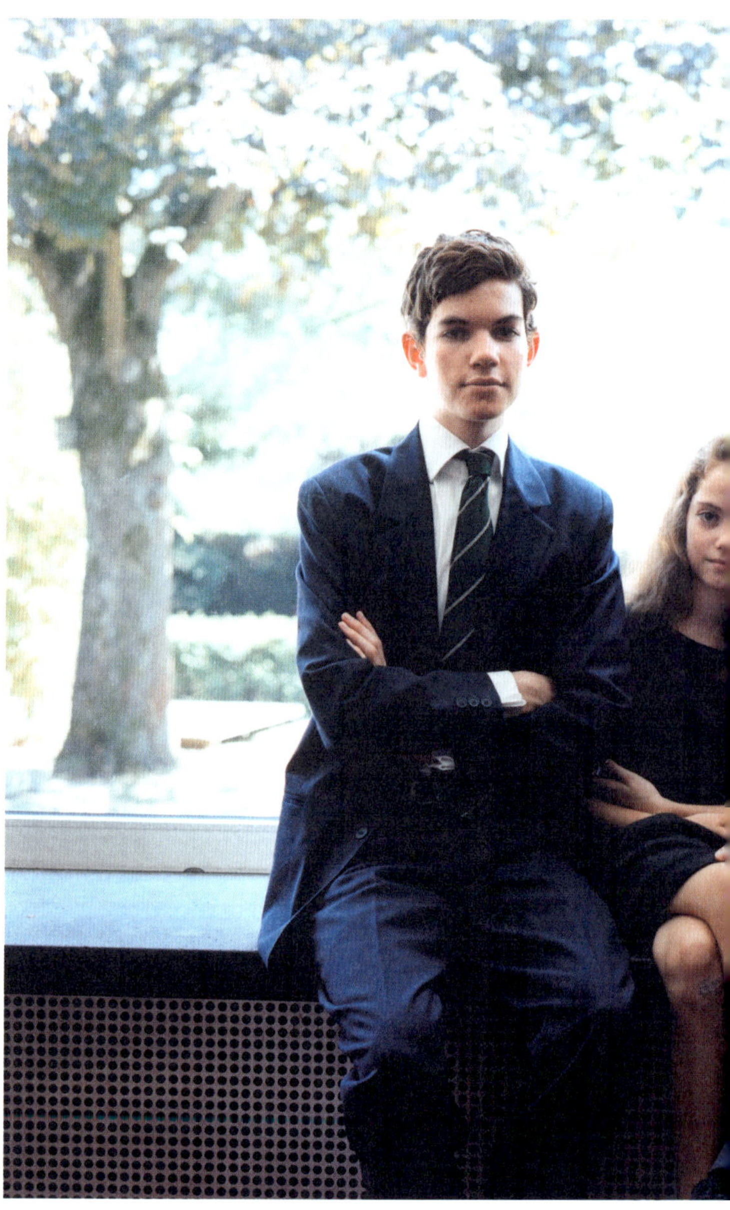

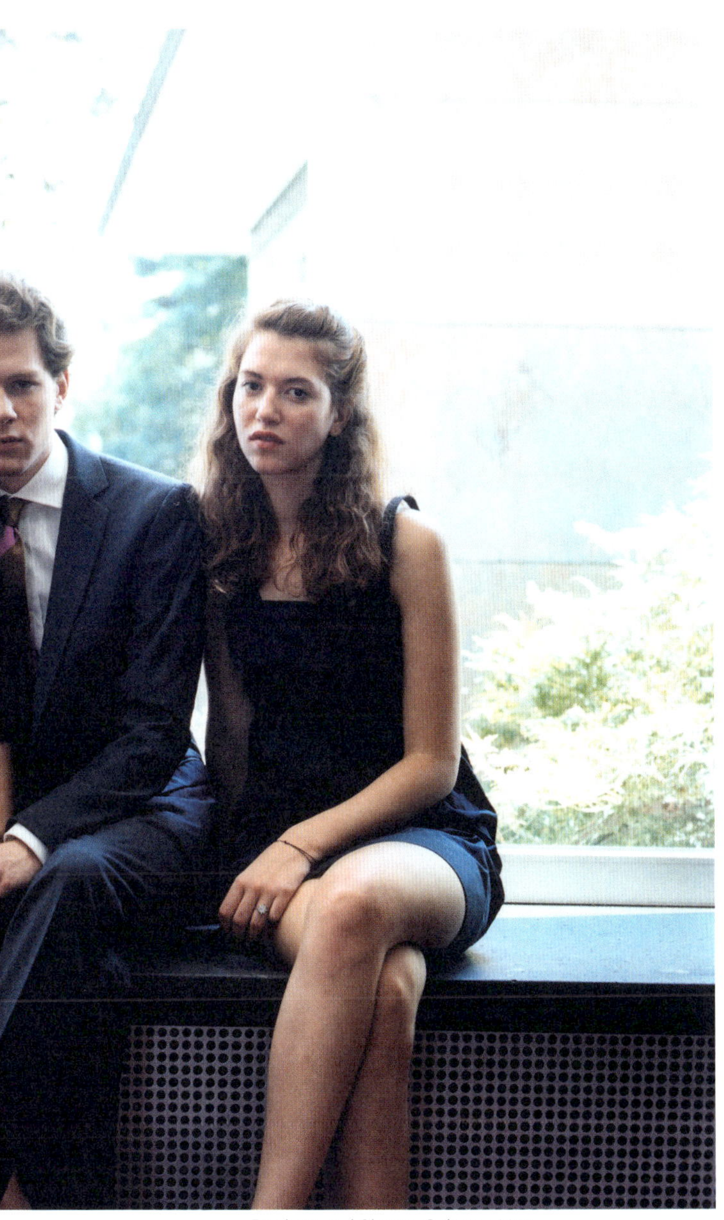

Brothers and Sisters, Cologne 2010

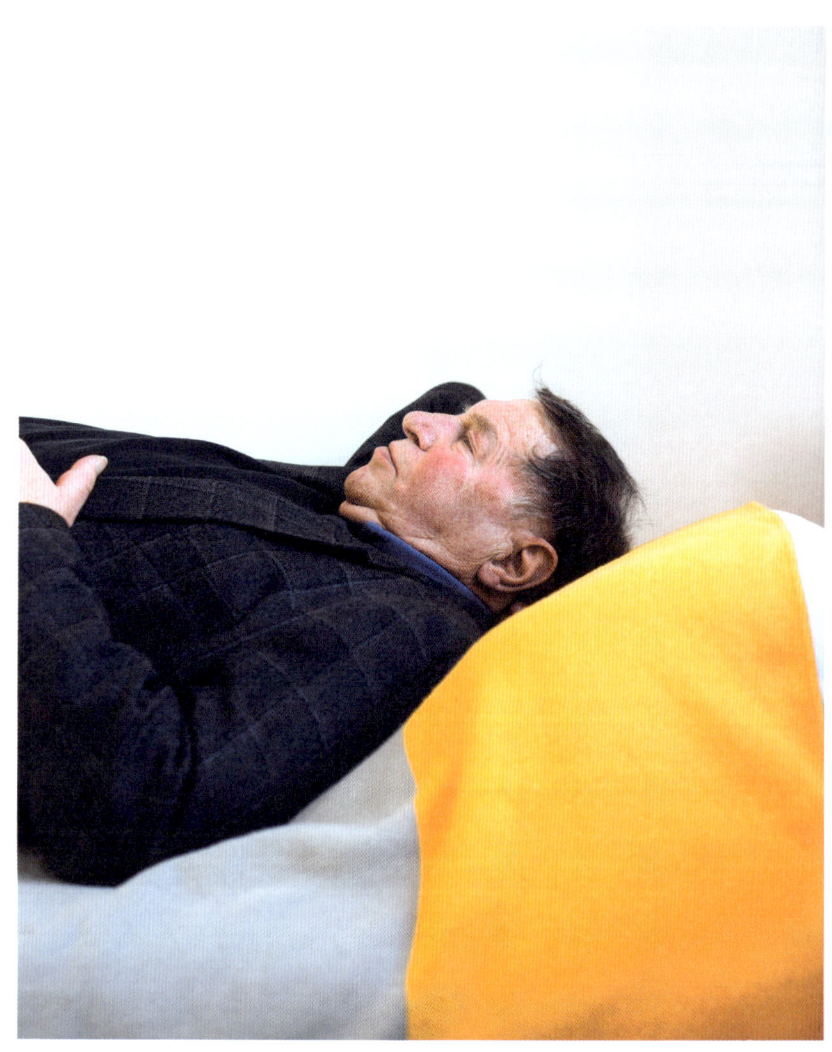

Franz Erhard Walther, Artist, Fulda 2013

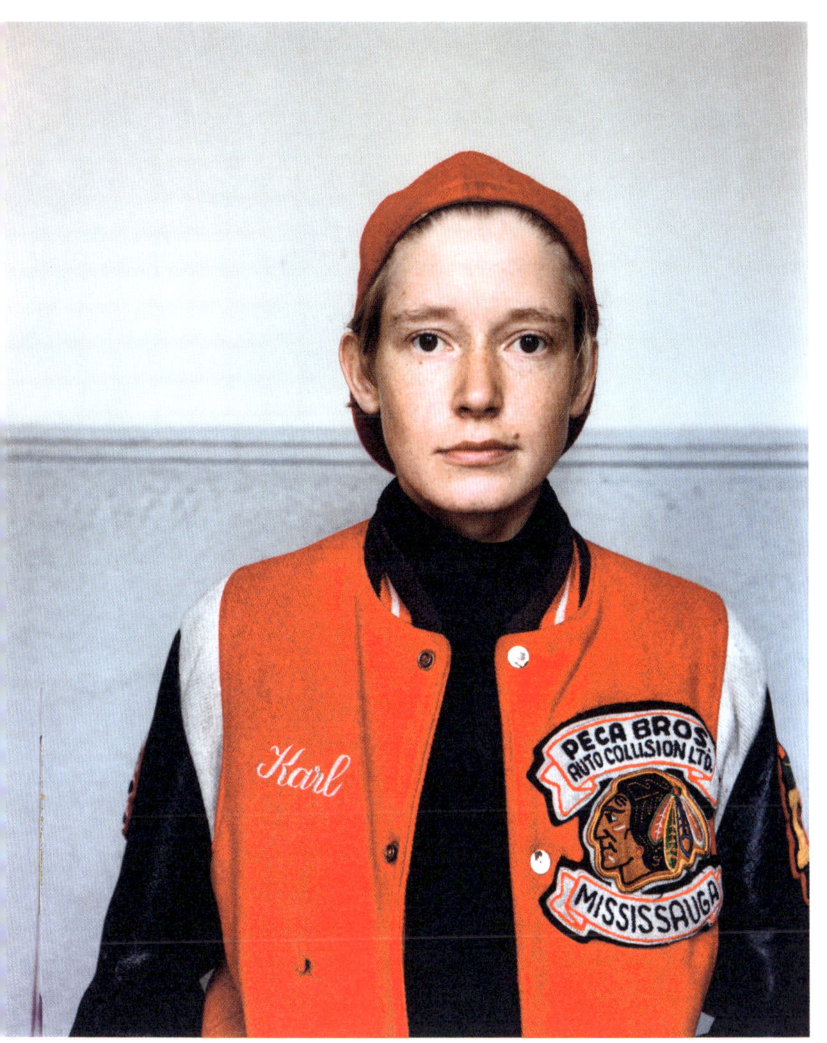

Antje Dorn, Artist, Düsseldorf 1990

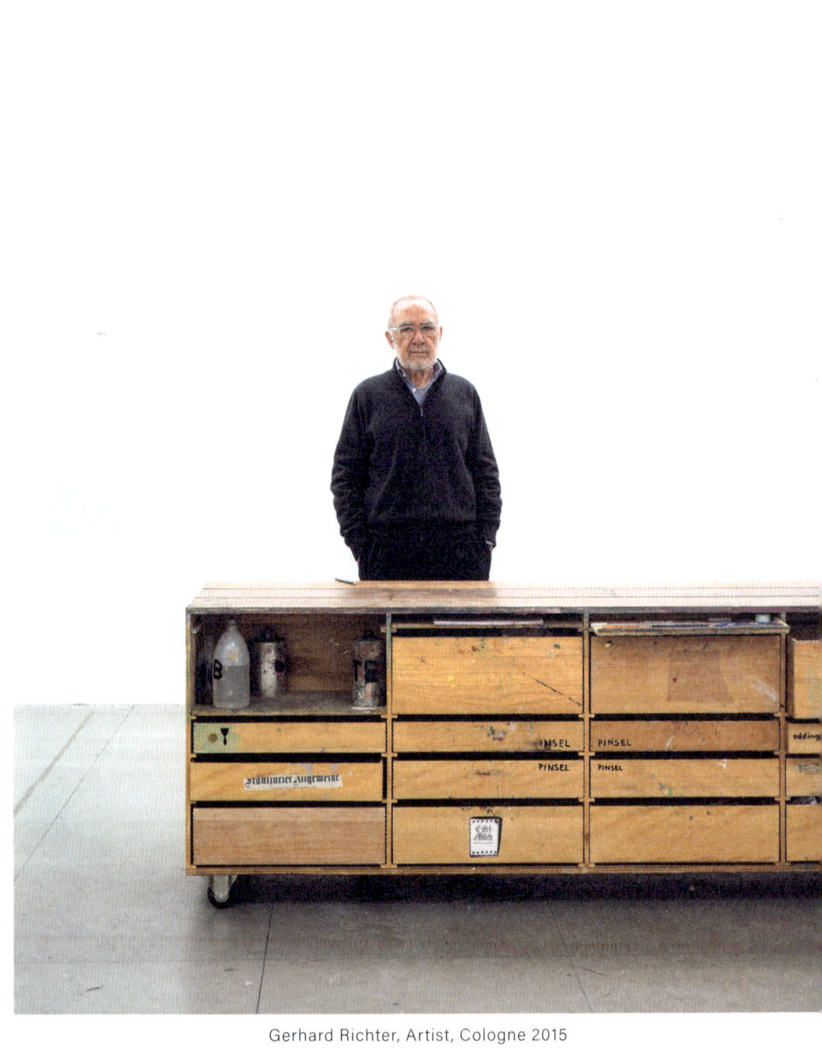

Gerhard Richter, Artist, Cologne 2015

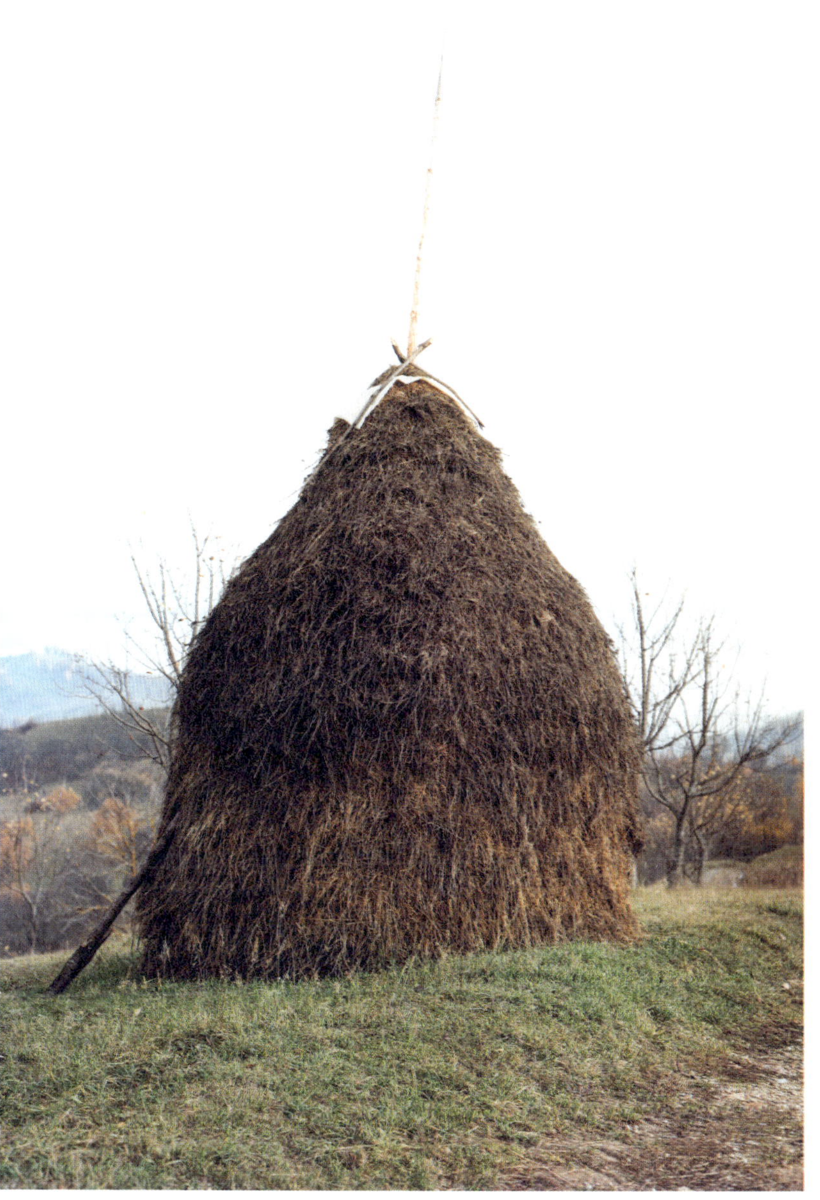

Haystack, Romania 2009

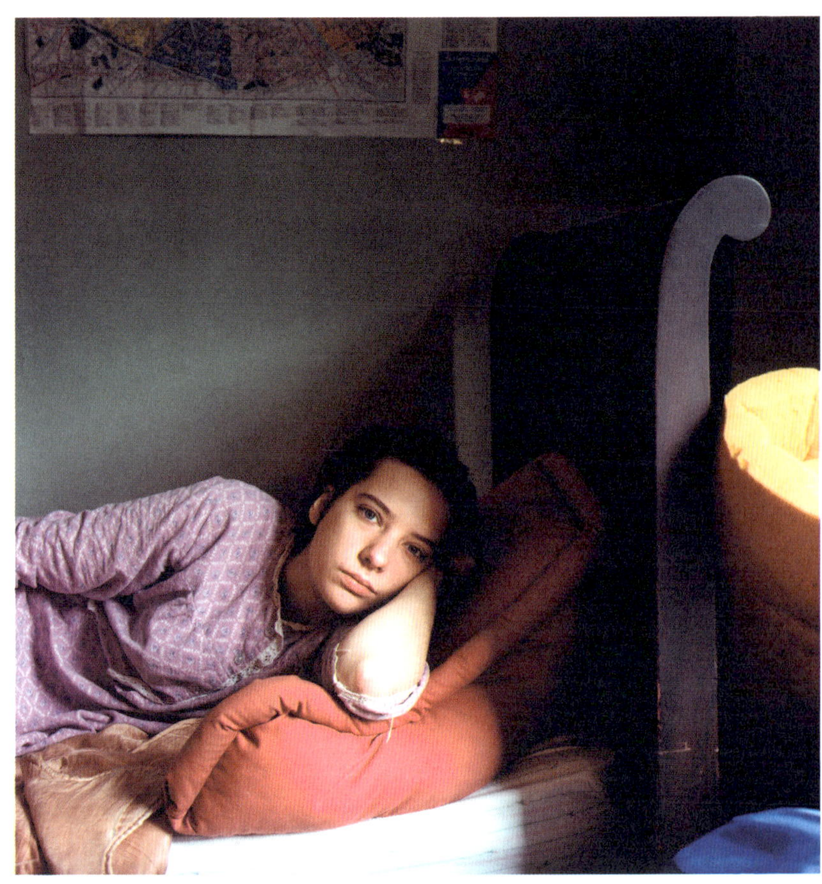

Leah Heineman, New York City 1989

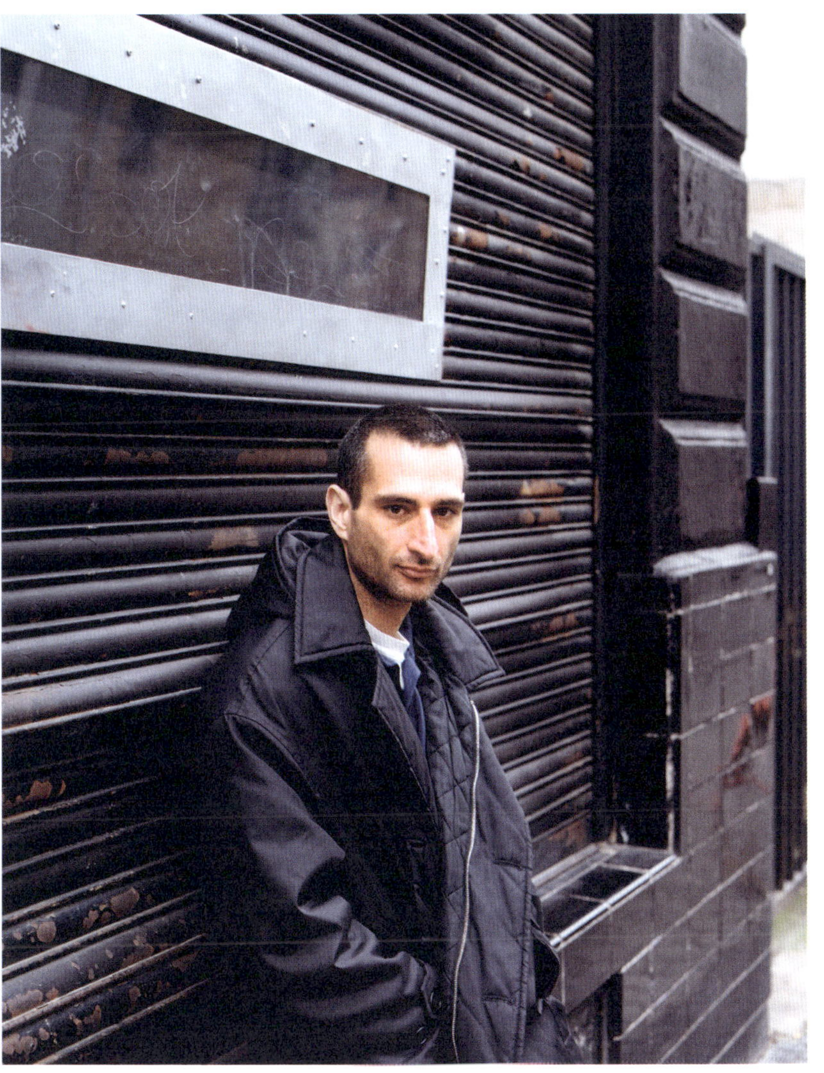

Christopher Wool, Artist, Cologne 1996

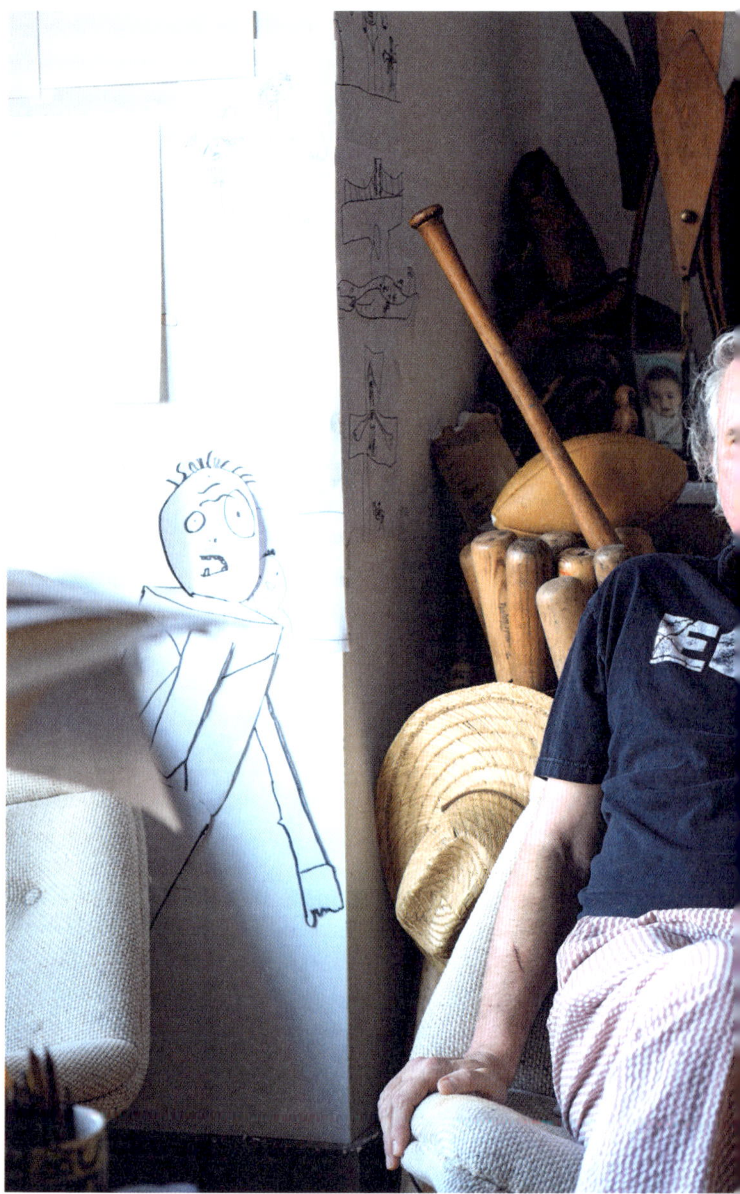

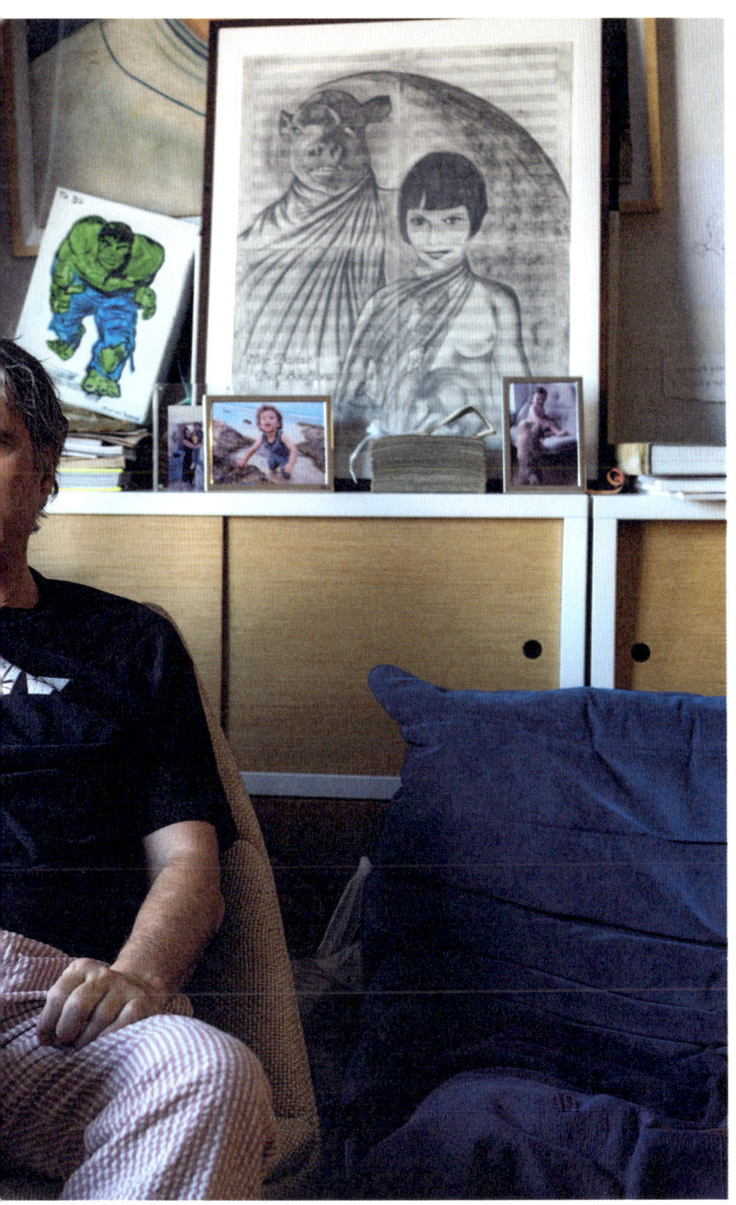

Raymond Pettibon, Artist, New York City 2018

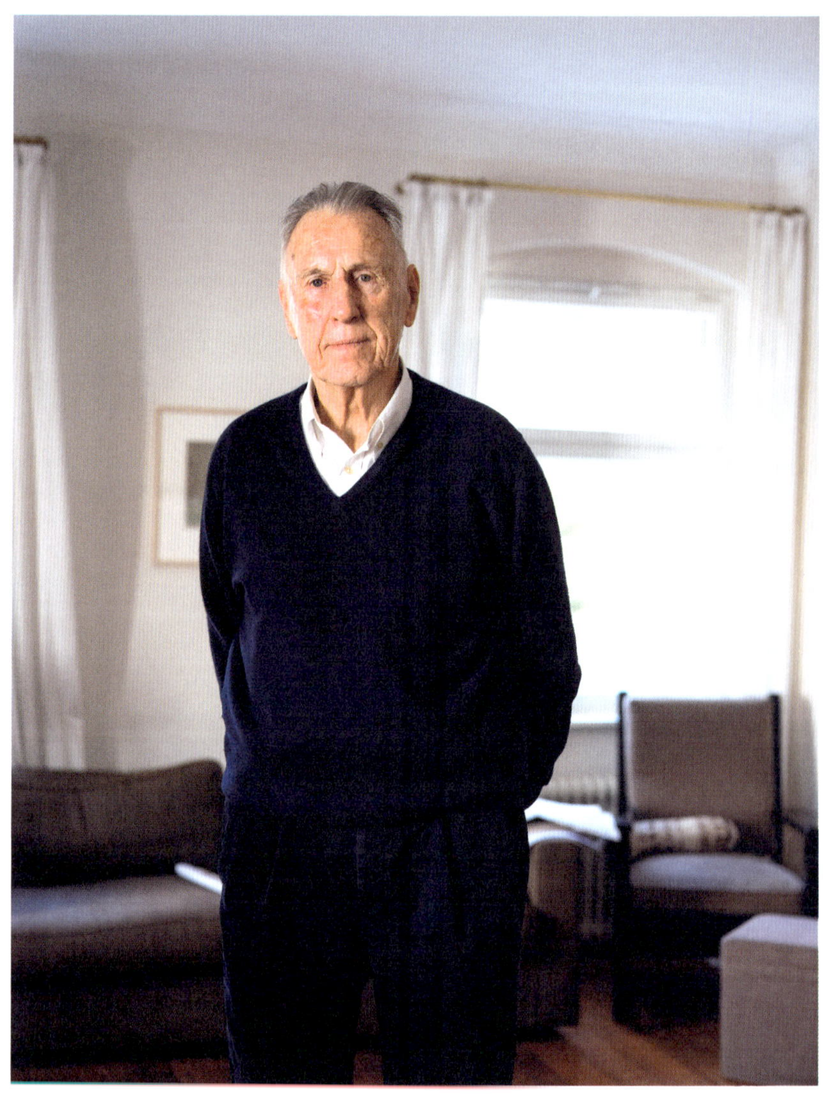

Rudolf Zwirner, Art Dealer, Berlin 2018

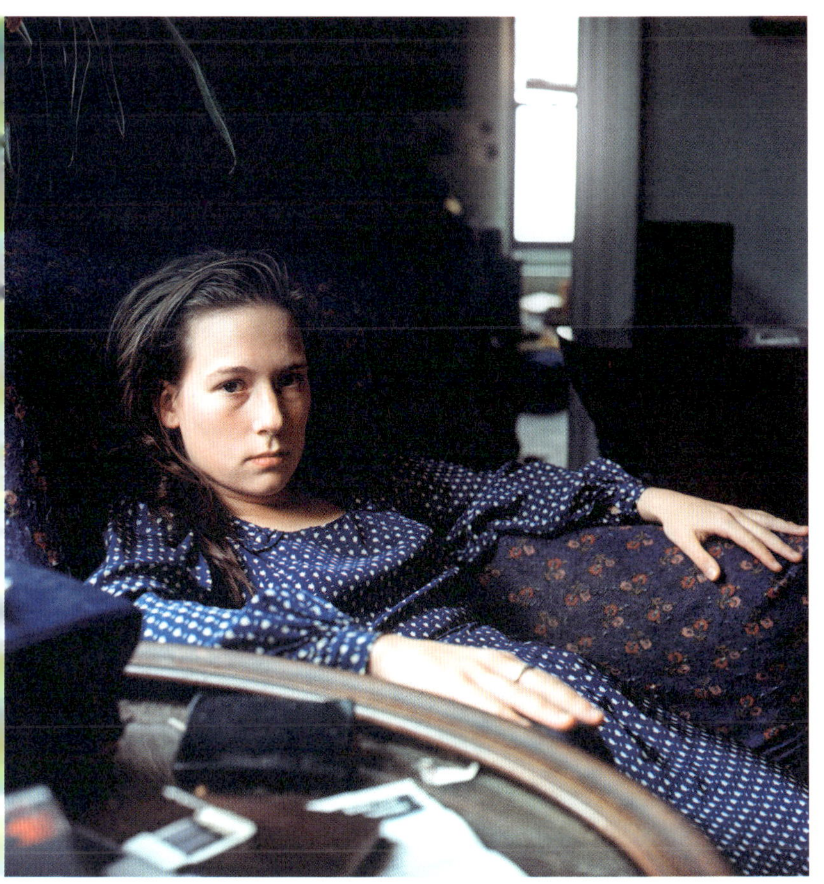

Rachel Heineman, Musican, New York City 1989

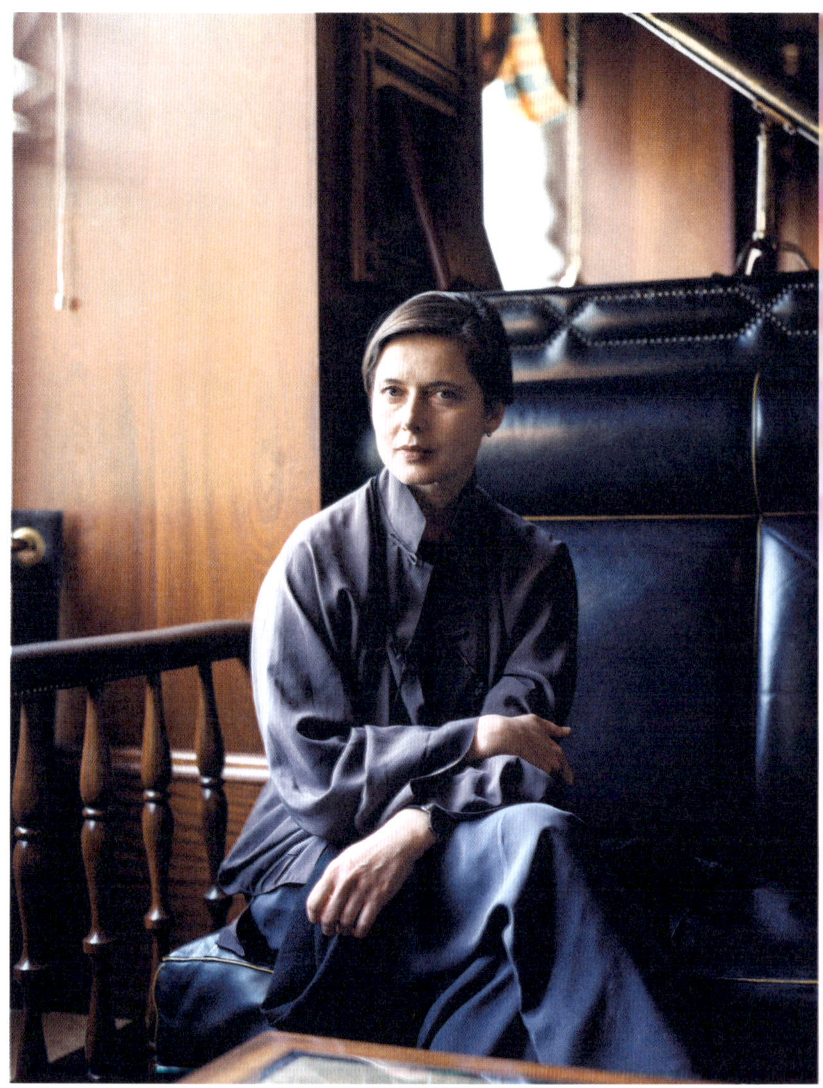

Isabella Rosselini, Actress, Düsseldorf 2002

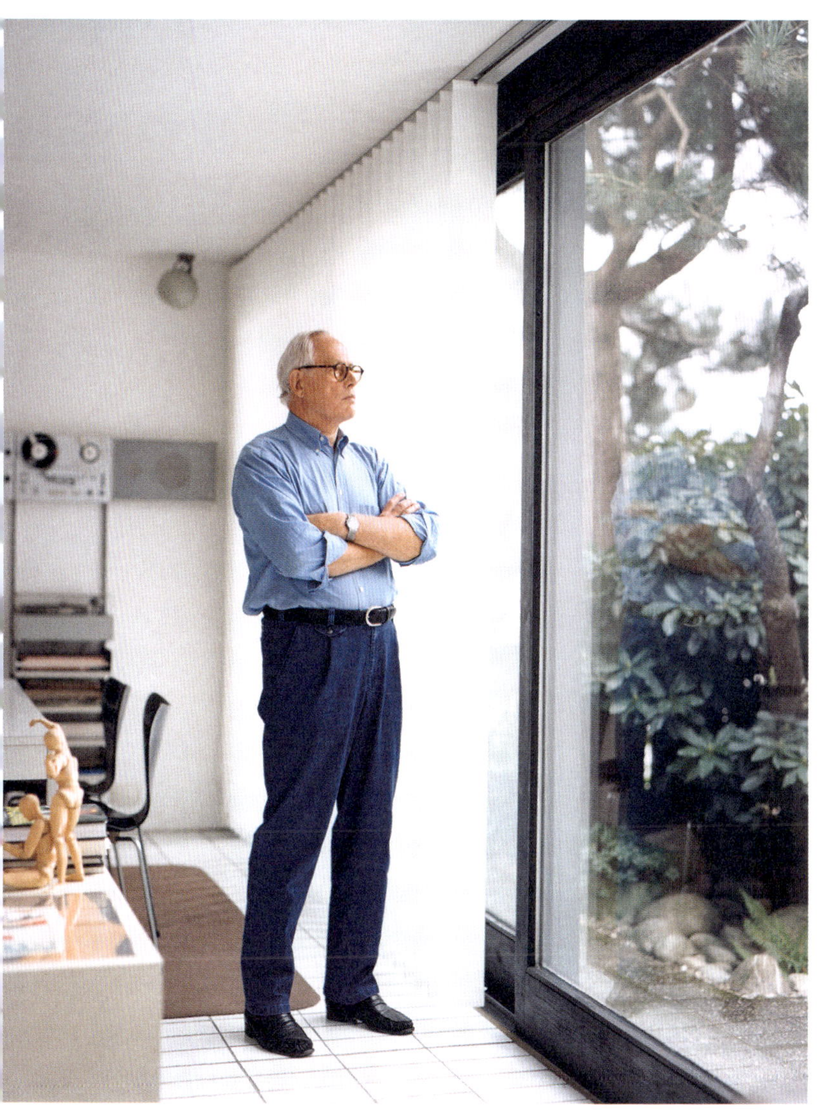

Dieter Rams, Industrial Designer, Kronberg 2001

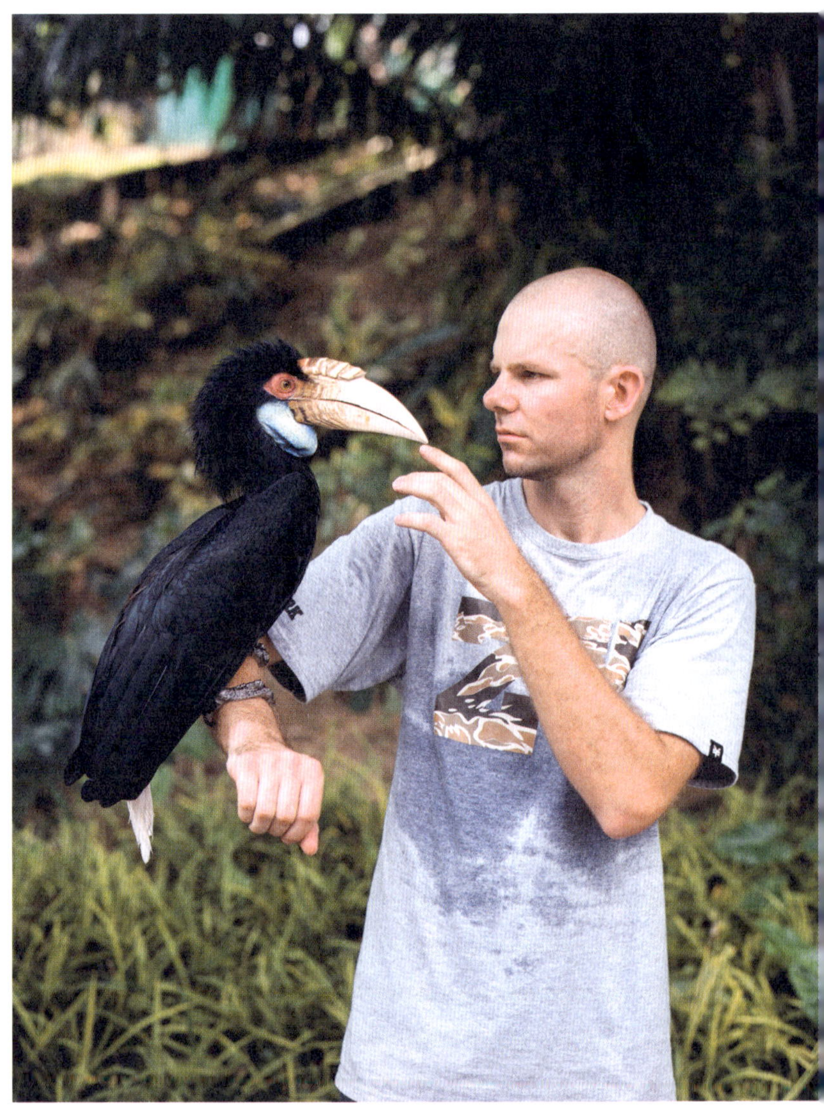

Shaun Gladwell, Artist, Kuala Lumpur 2005

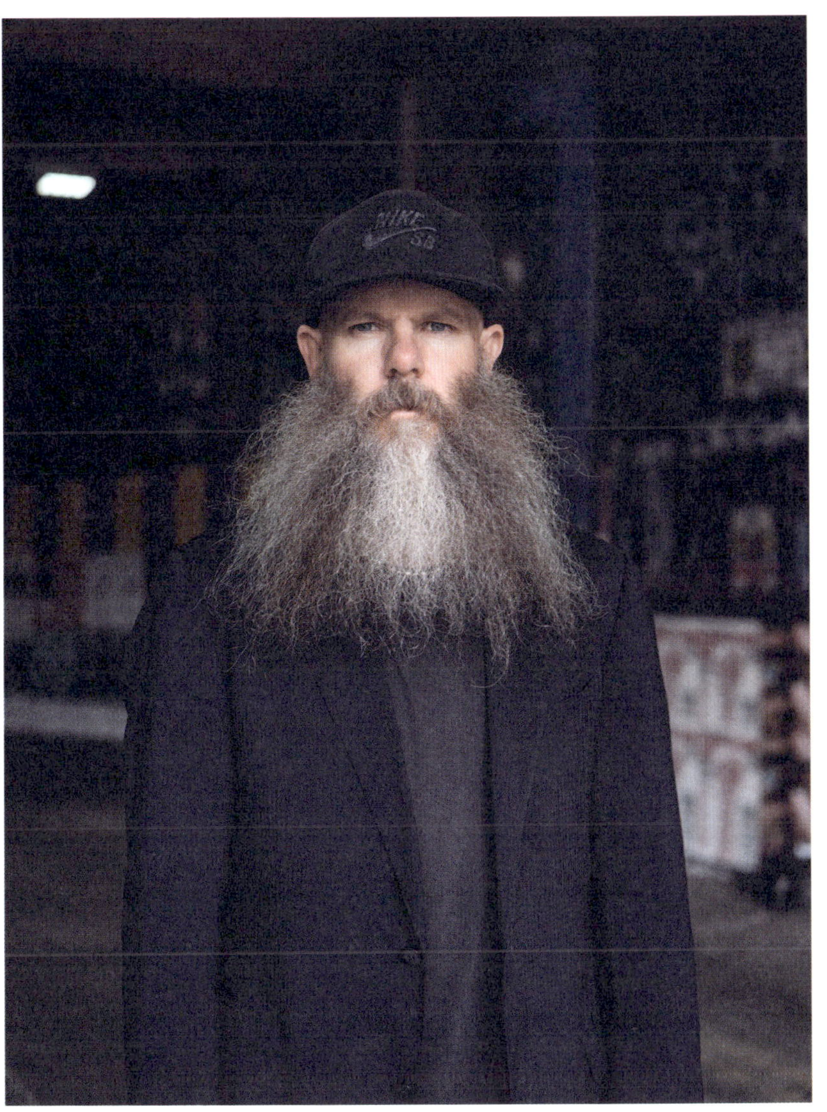

Shaun Gladwell, Artist, London 2018

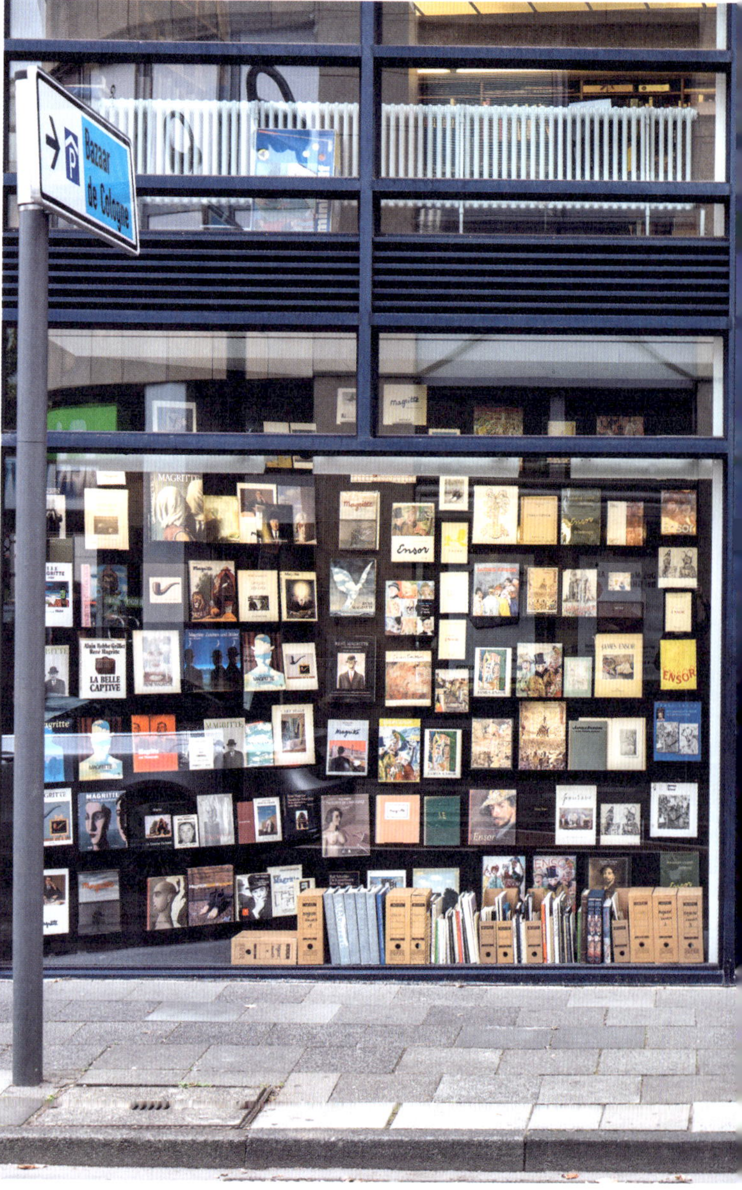
Bazaar
de Cologne
MAGRITTE
Ensor
Alain Robbe-Grillet
René Magritte
LA BELLE
CAPTIVE
JAMES ENSOR
ENSOR

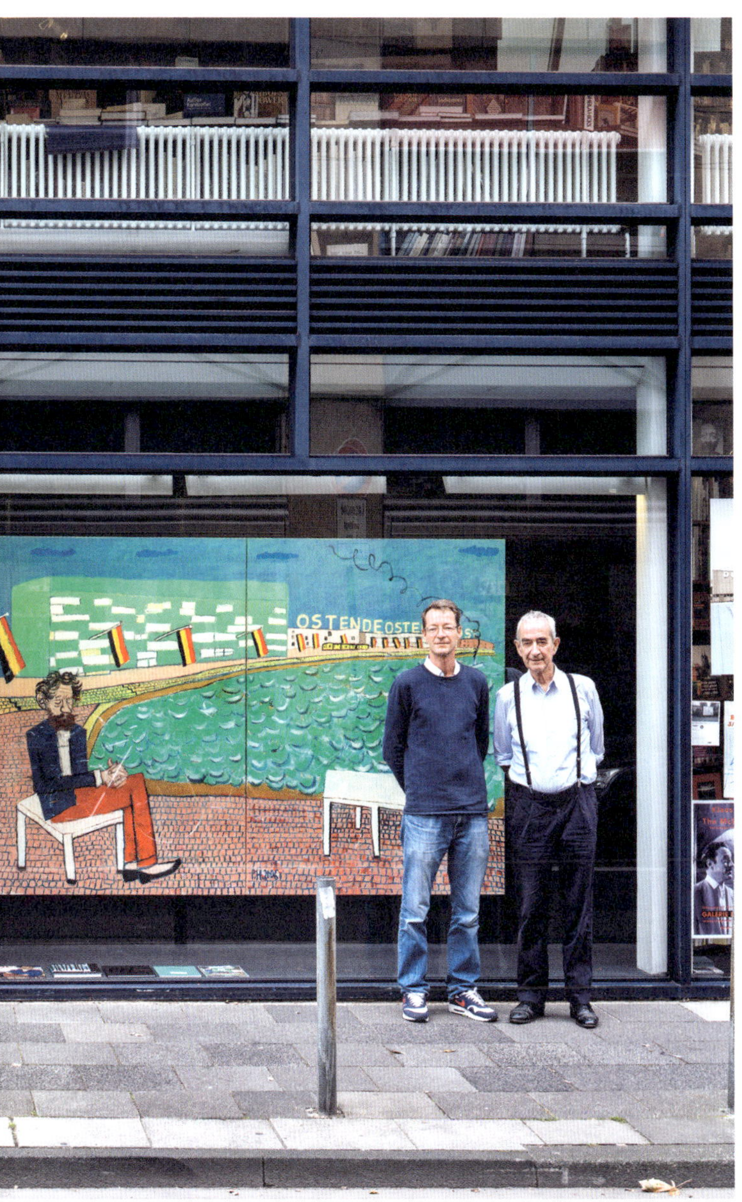

Franz König and Walther König, Publishers and Booksellers, Cologne 2019

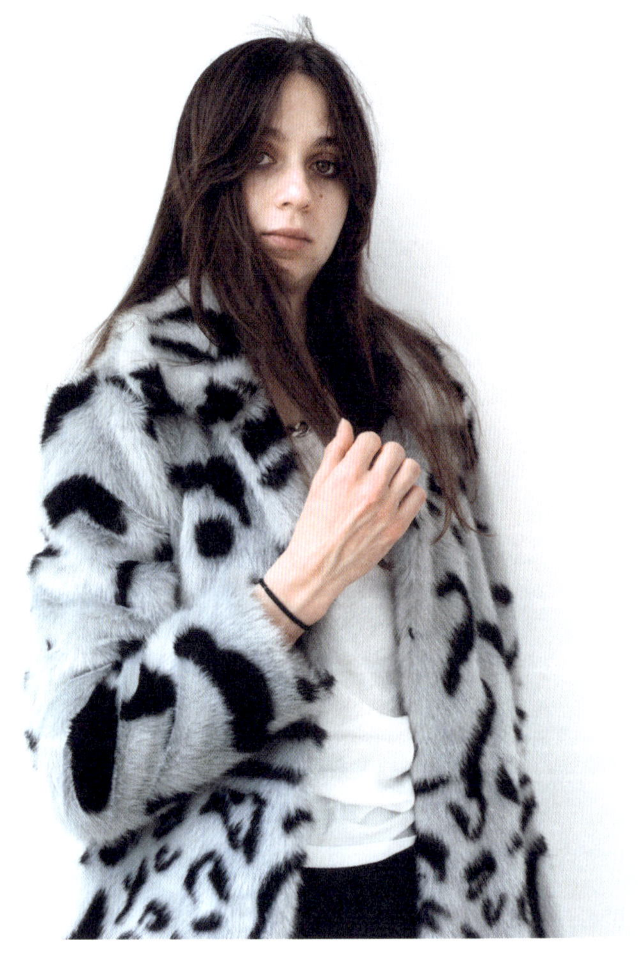

Avery Singer, Artist, Cologne 2017

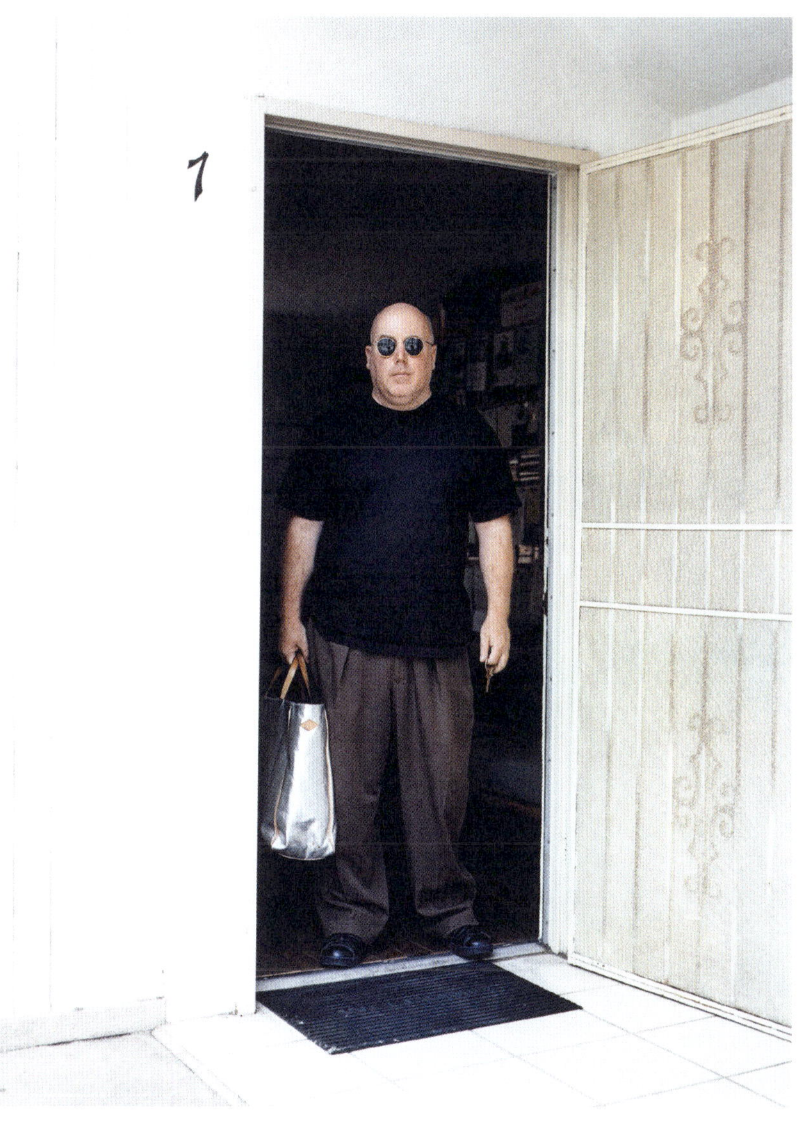

Christopher Williams, Artist, Los Angeles 2004

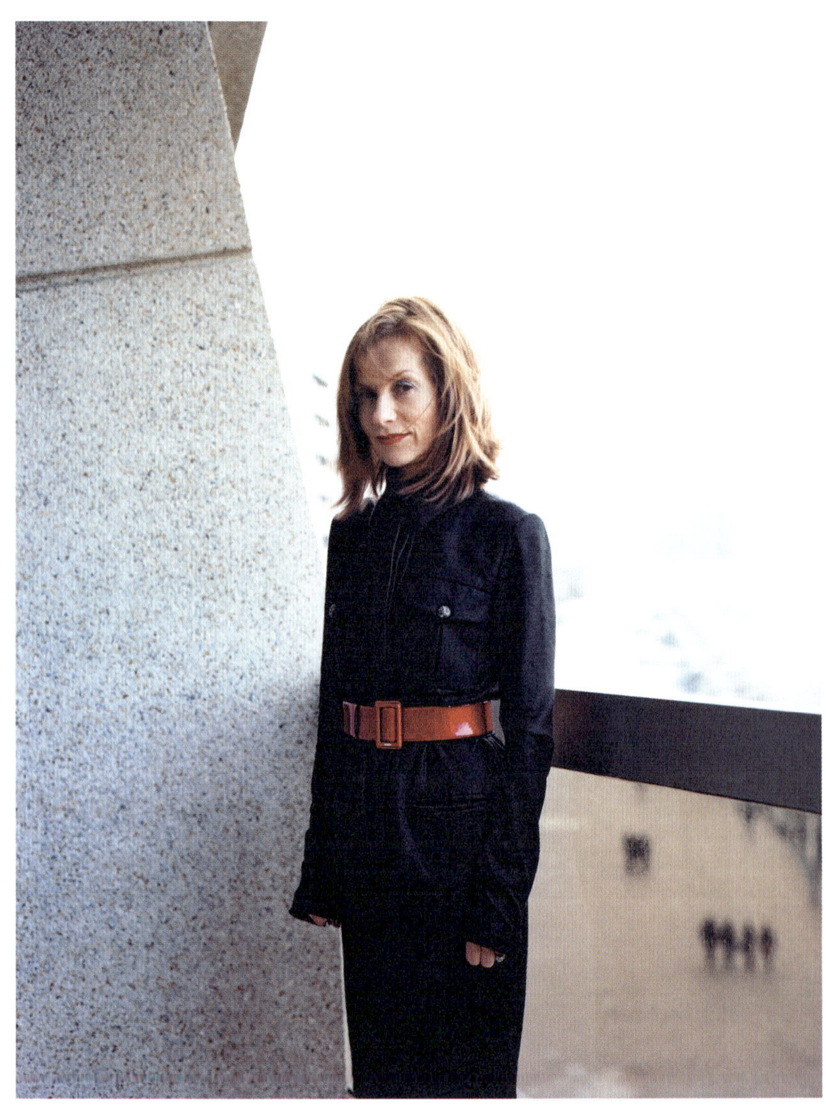

Isabelle Huppert, Actress, Oostende 2009

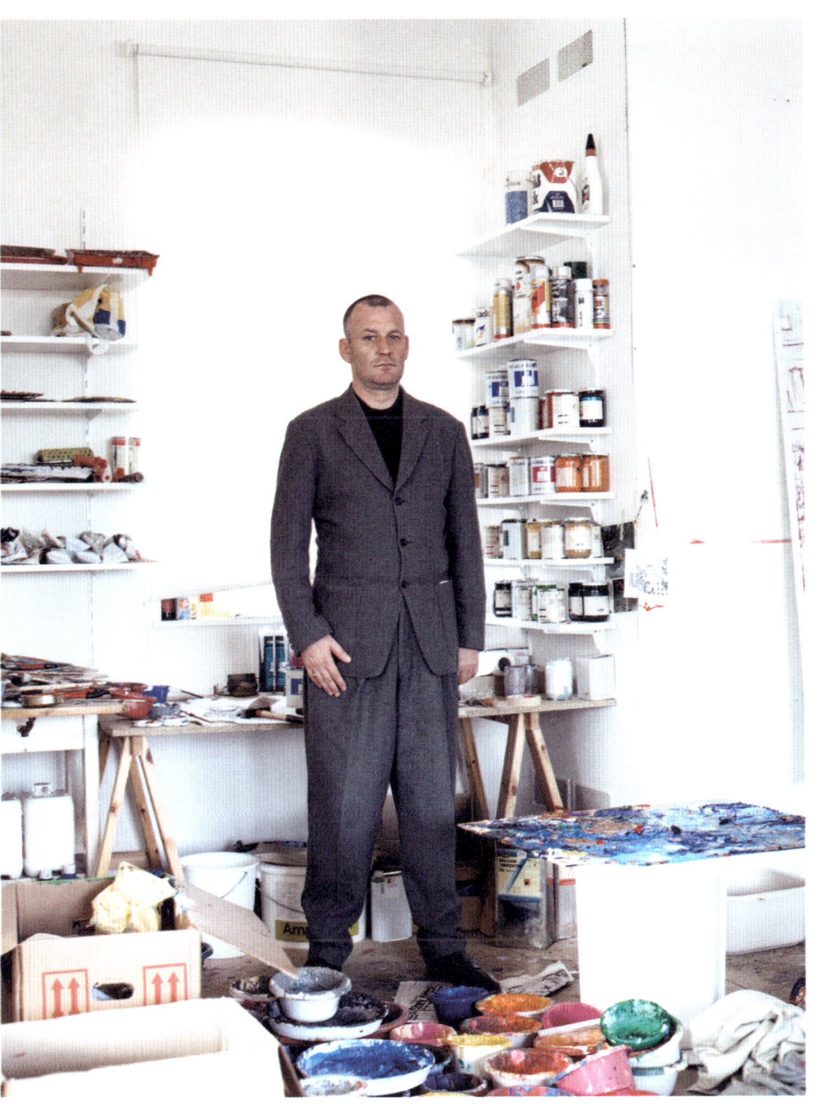

Martin Kippenberger, Artist, St. Georgen/Germany 1995

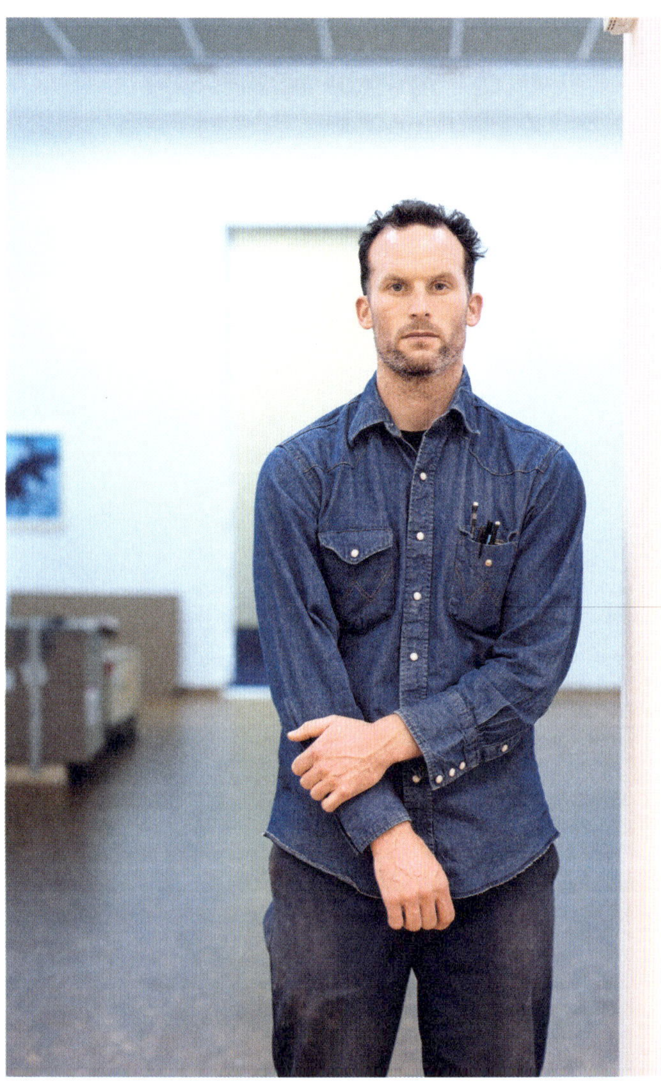

Matthew Barney, Artist, Cologne 2002

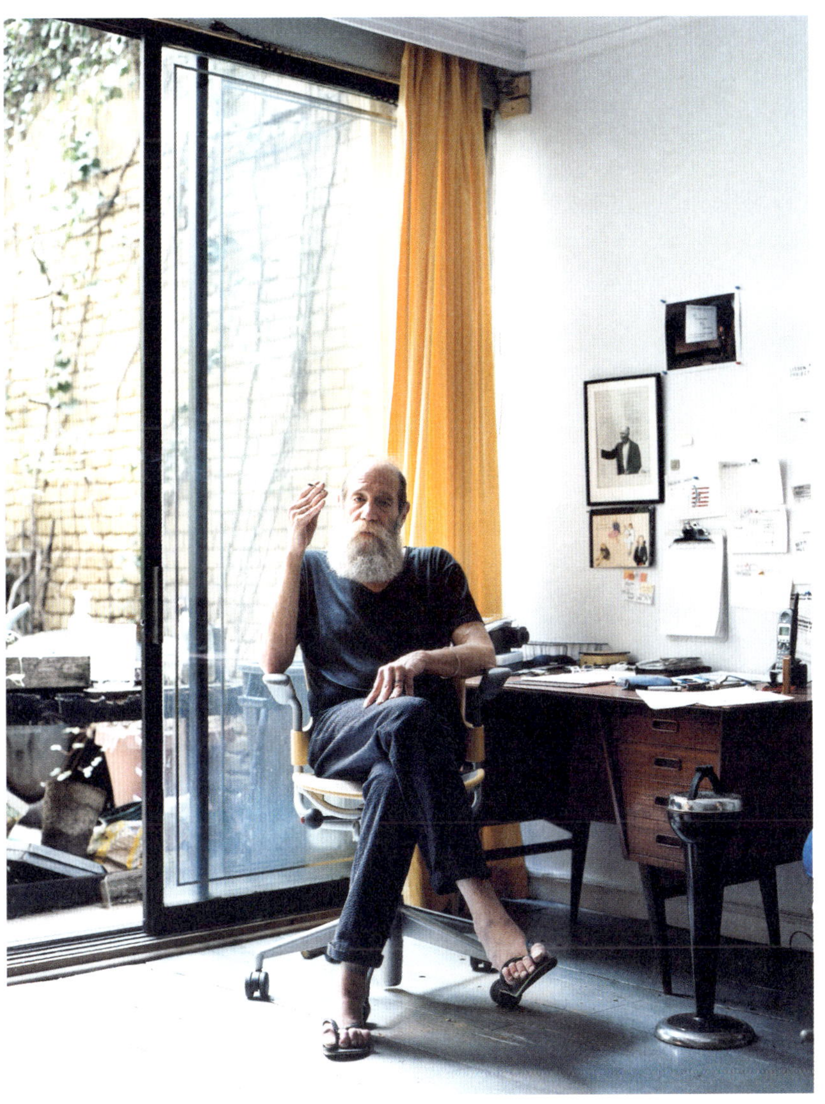

Lawrence Weiner, Artist, New York City 2005

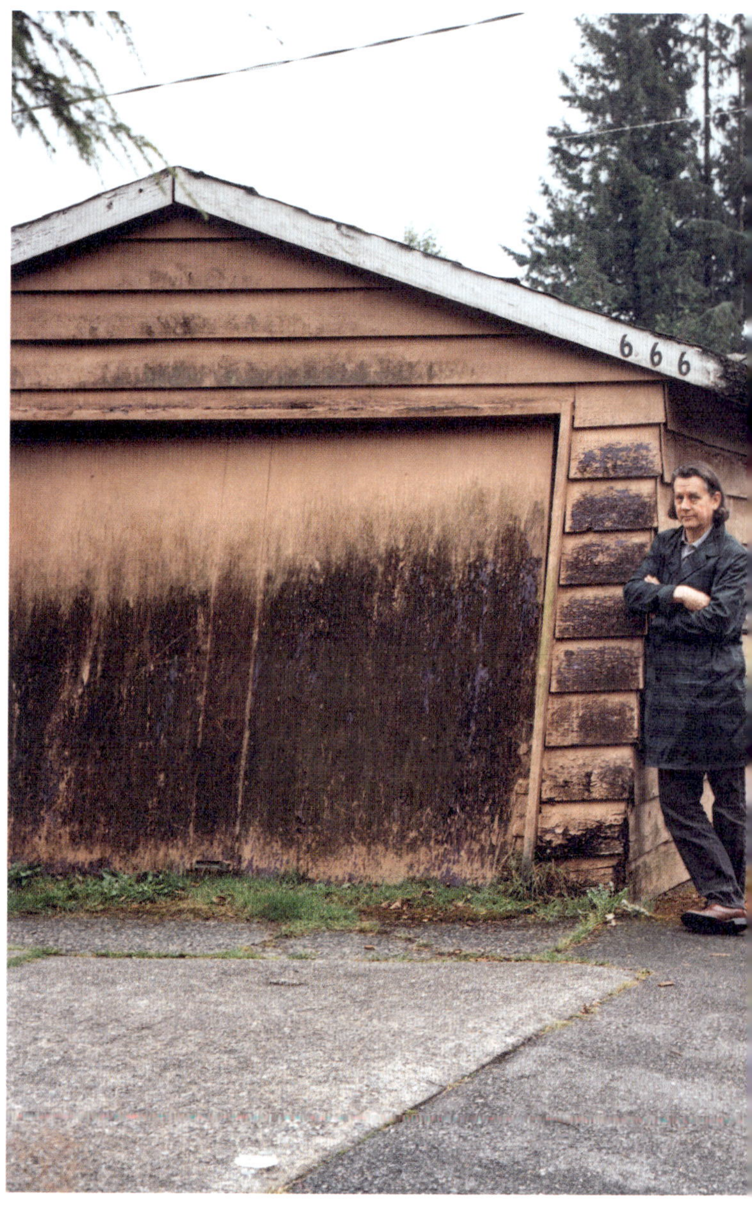
666

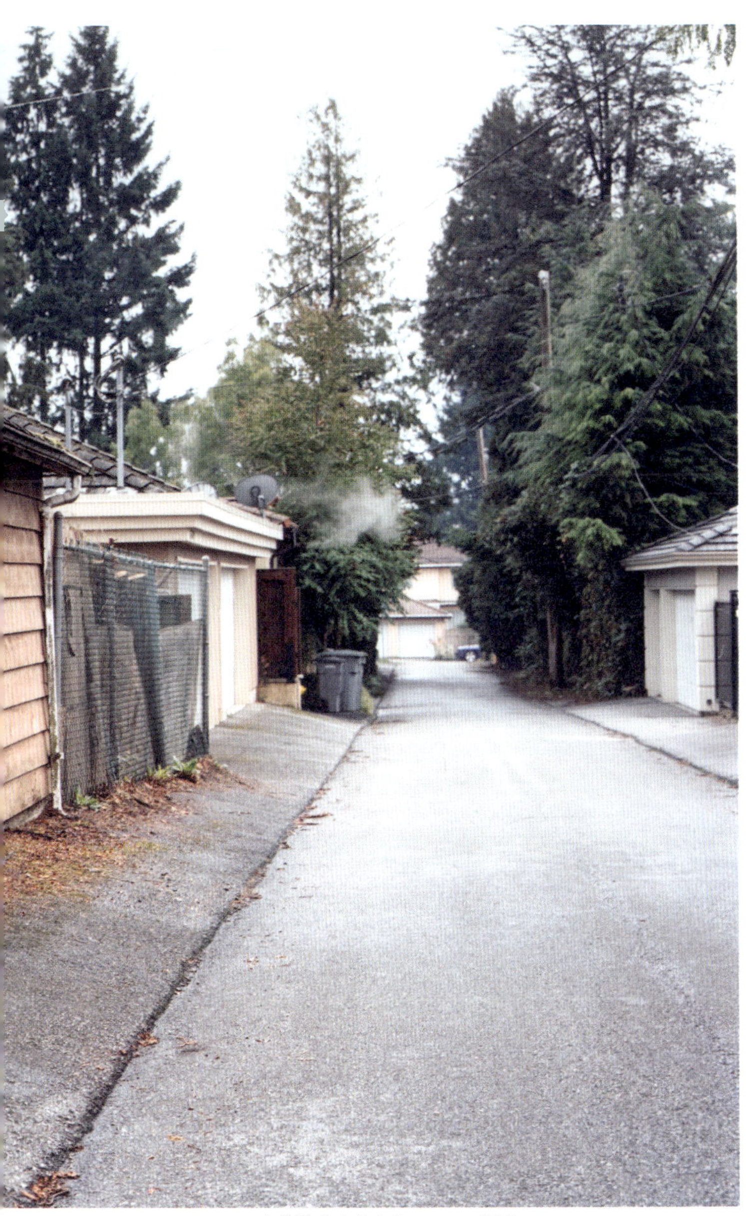

Jeff Wall, Artist, Vancouver 2010

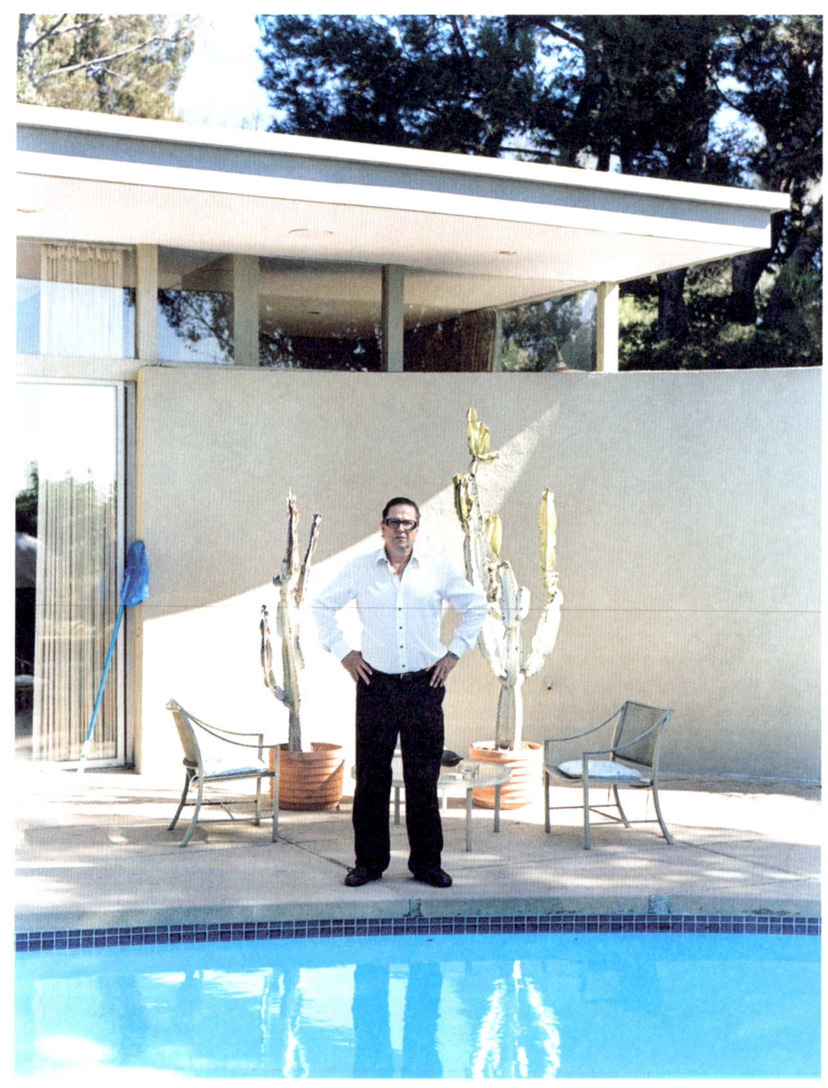

Georg Herold, Artist, Los Angeles 2005

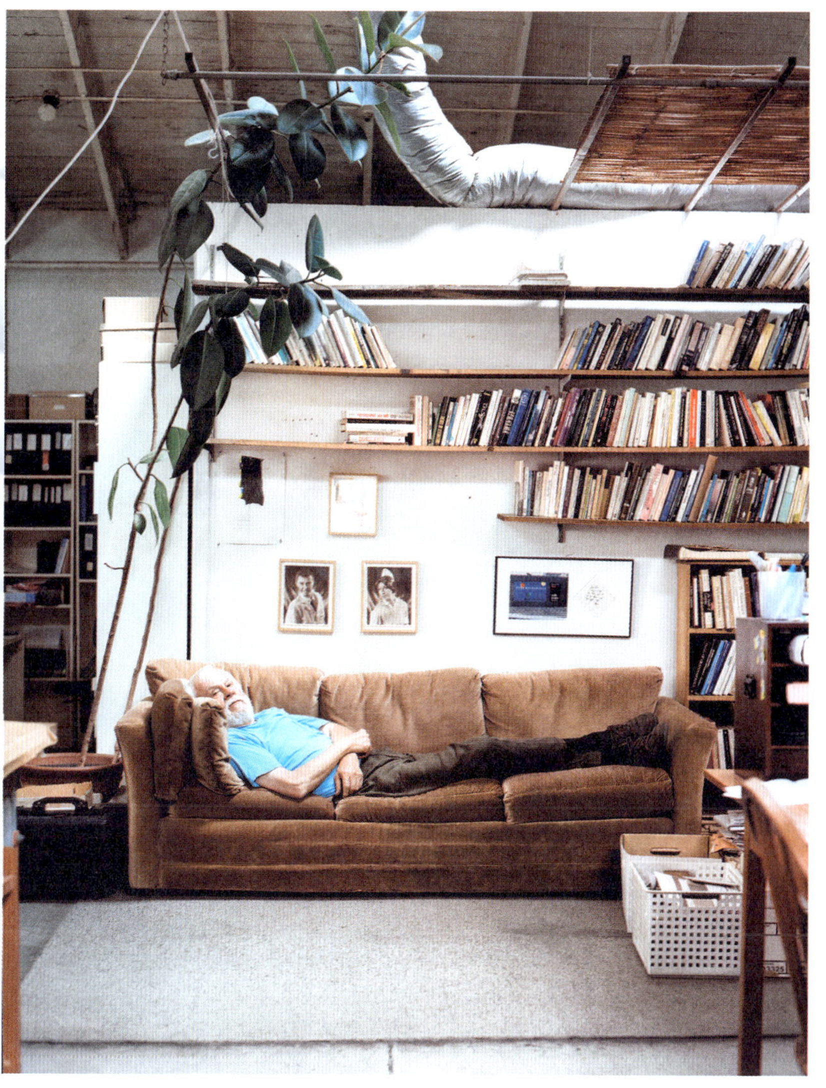

John Baldessari, Artist, Los Angeles 2004

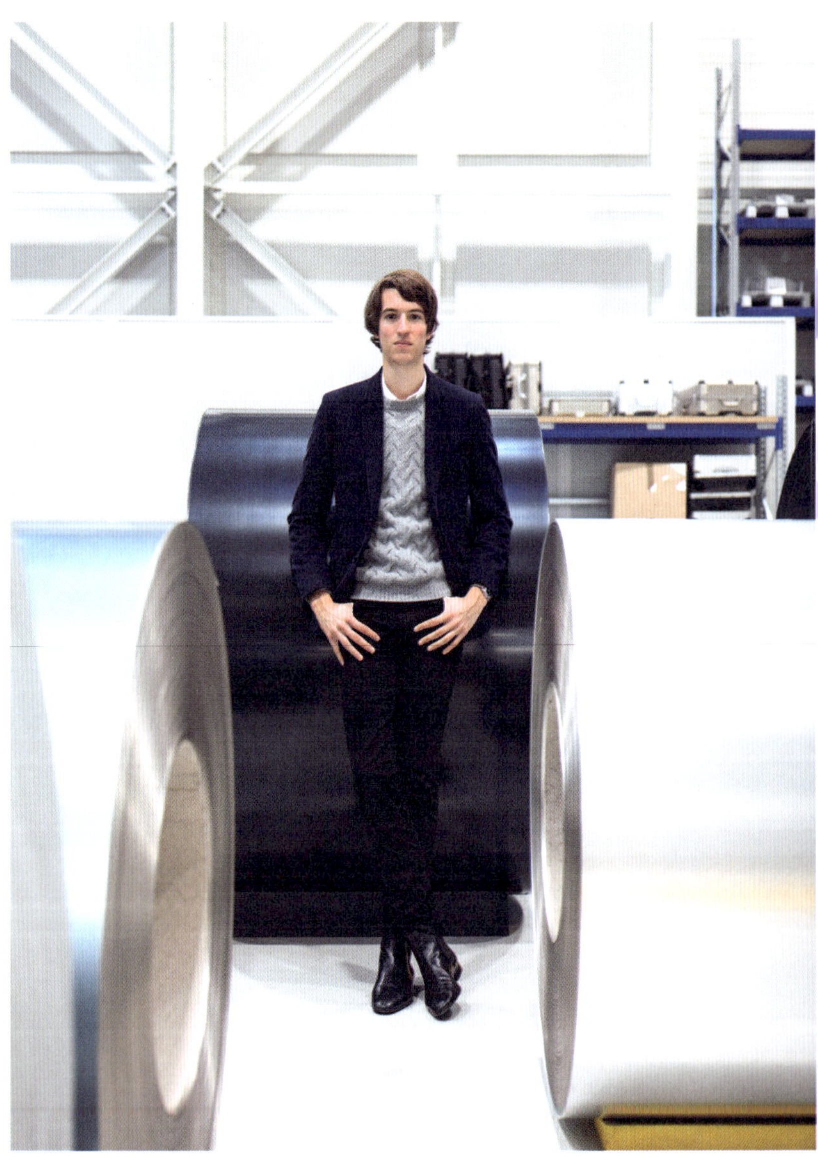

Alexander Arnault, Entrepreneur, Cologne 2018

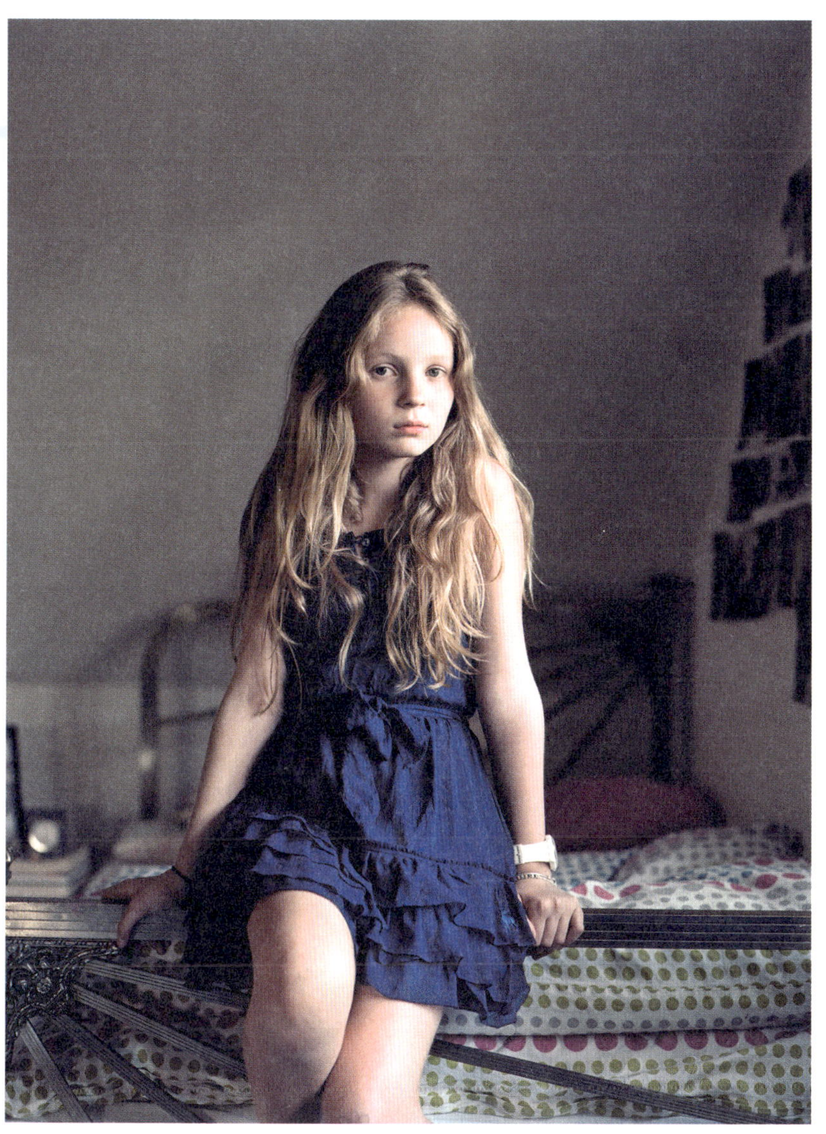

Bella Brunnet, Berlin 2012

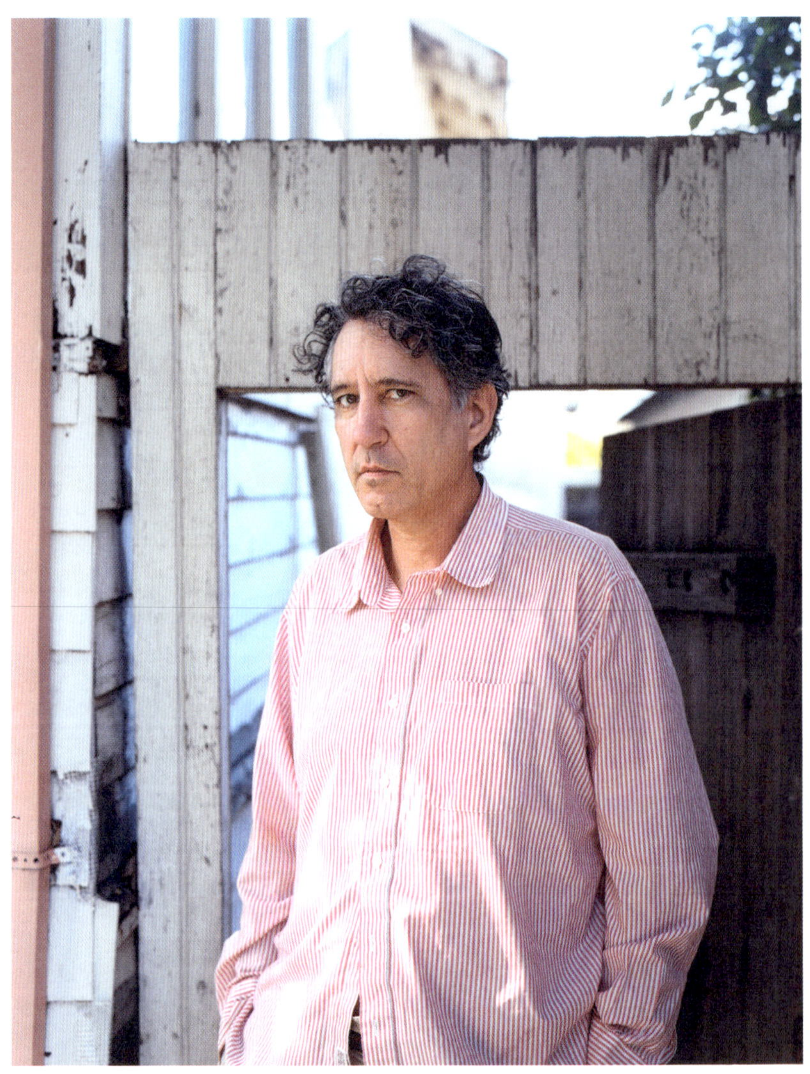

Raymond Pettibon, Artist, Los Angeles 2008

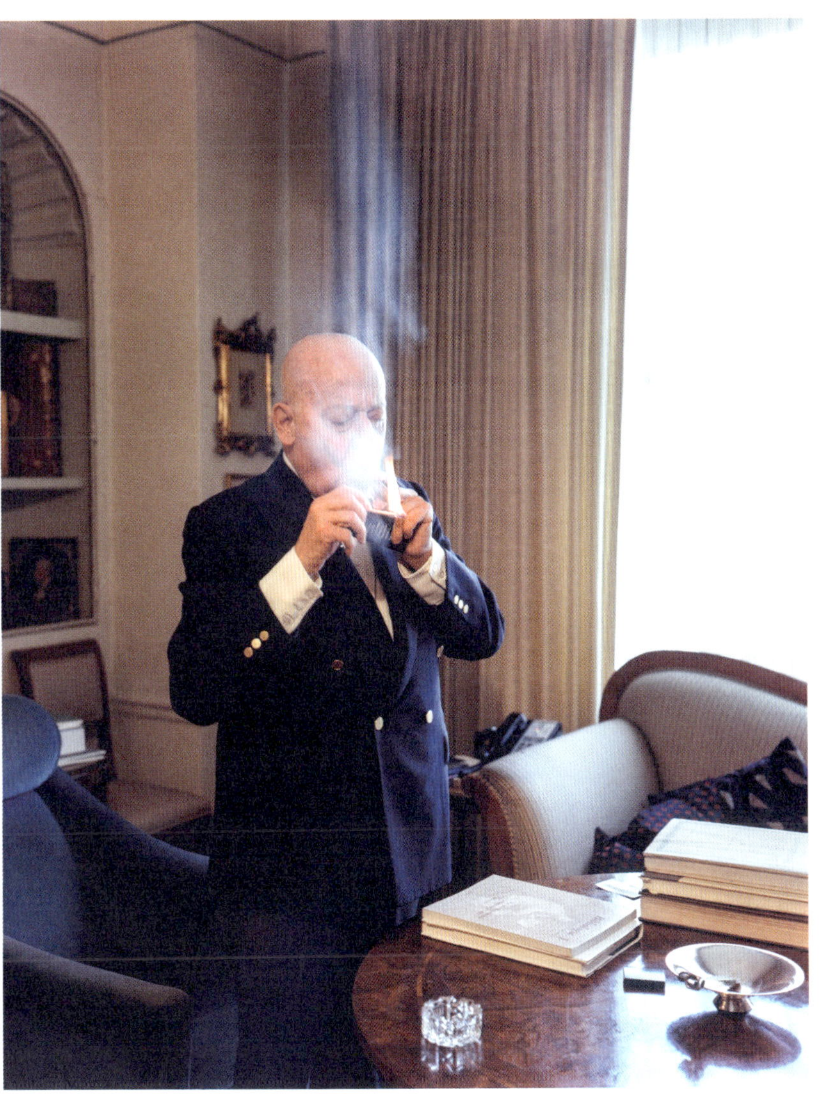

Bernard H. Breslauer, Antiquarian Bookdealer, New York City 1993

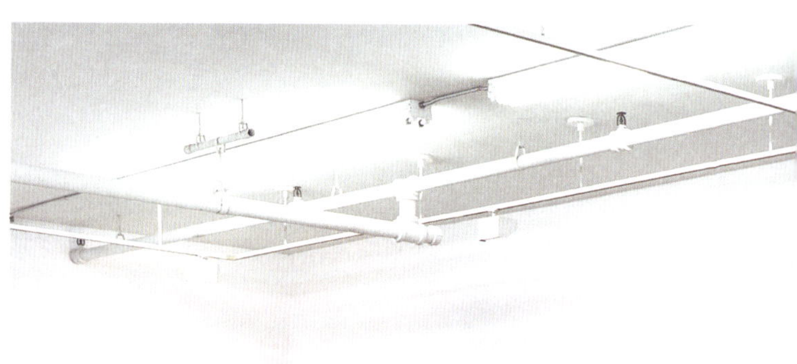

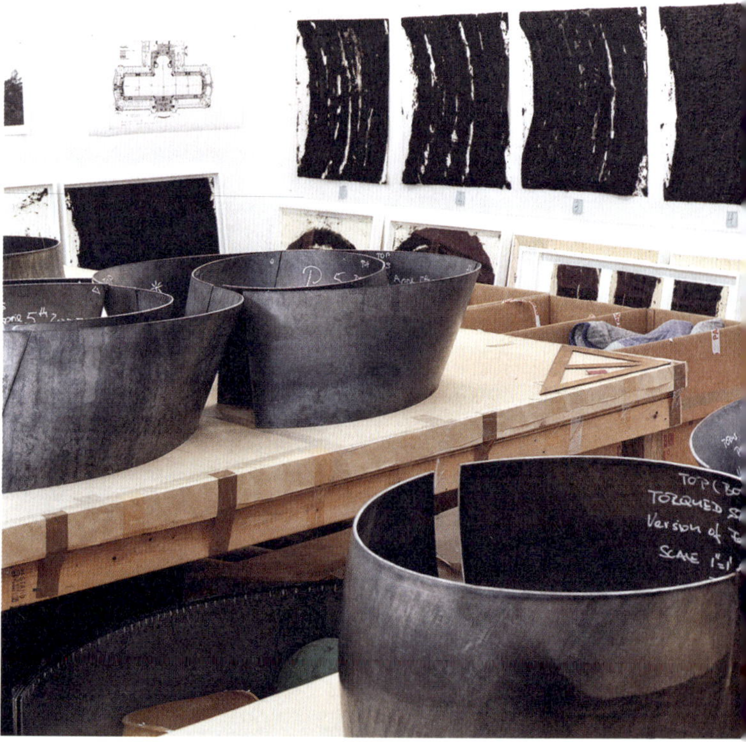

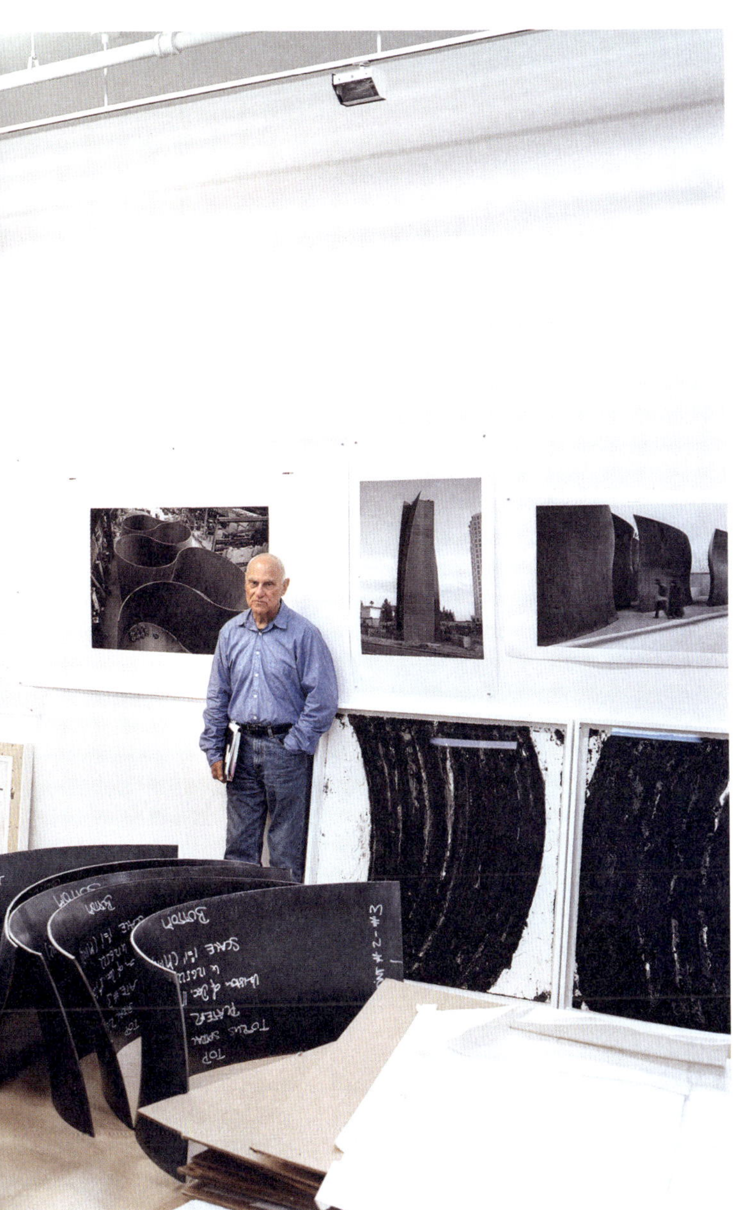

Richard Serra, Artist, New York City 2007

Albrecht Fuchs Fifty-Three Portraits and a Haystack Albrecht Fuchs is a *Heimlifeister*, a Swiss-German expression that means that someone can do more than he wants to show. He doesn't let you look into his cards, he doesn't talk much and he doesn't bluff. But for three decades he has been taking the most wonderful portraits of artists and outstanding protagonists of the cultural world; he practically goes in and out in their studios and ateliers and for reasons unknown to me, he has access to their soul—I don't know how he does it. Because soul, at least glimpses of it, are shown to us in these photographs; the pictures speak, Albrecht doesn't have to speak much himself. But he must have a great love for the artists, probably he himself is an artist's soul, but this should not be confused with an absolute claim to art. He does exhibit his works in renowned galleries, but—with respect—it is still photography, real, "normal" photography, honest and dry, and without frills. There was hardly the urge or the vision to become and to be a big photo artist à la Ruff Gursky Struth, at least that's my impression. There everything has already been grazed and sold up to the very last and somehow demystified. Fuchs works, so to speak, in silence, year after year, job after job, teaches here and there and does mainly free work again and again—which I suppose is his favourite thing. He simply likes to be with artists, in their aura, with their works and possibly the smell of paint (in Richter's case, for example). And you can just see that in these photographs, you feel that they are really good, but you don't know exactly why, you can't really crack the secret of this photographer. Do you even want to? When I started to get to know and love photography, I was deeply fascinated by the pictures of August Sander—my girlfriend at that time was a booksellers apprentice and gave me the wonderful Schirmer edition of *Menschen des 20. Jahrhunderts*—each picture a rich document and it is highly exciting to look so closely at people from a different era, to observe them. I don't think it is presumptuous at all to place Albrecht Fuchs in the same tradition, and I naturally hope that in fifty years a young person will take this small book into their hands and feel the same happiness by being part of the family of man as well as of the essence of the artistic.

Albrecht Fuchs Fifty-Three Portraits and a Haystack Albrecht Fuchs ist ein *Heimlifeister*, das ist ein schweizerdeutscher Ausdruck, der sagen will, dass einer mehr kann als er zeigen will. Er lässt sich nichts anmerken, spricht nicht viel und prahlt nicht herum. Er photographiert aber seit drei Dekaden die herrlichsten Portraits von Künstlern und herausragenden Protagonisten der Kulturwelt; er geht quasi bei Ihnen ein und aus und hat aus mir unbekannten Gründen Zugang zu Ihrer Seele, ich weiss echt nicht wie er es macht. Denn Seele, zumindest Zipfel davon, zeigen uns diese Bilder, die Bilder sprechen, Albrecht muss gar nichts sagen. Er muss aber eine grosse Liebe zu den Künstlern haben, vermutlich ist er selber eine Künstlerseele, was aber nicht verwechselt werden will mit absolutem Kunstanspruch. Er stellt zwar seine Bilder in renomierten Galerien aus, aber – mit Verlaub – es ist immer noch Photographie, richtige, „normale" Photographie, ehrlich und trocken und ohne Kinkerlitzchen. Aber eben, da war wohl kaum der Drang oder die Vision ein Grossphotokünstler à la Ruff Gursky Struth zu werden und zu sein, so ist zumindest mein Eindruck. Dort ist auch schon alles abgegrast und bis ins allerletzte verhökert und irgendwie auch entmystifiziert. Fuchs arbeitet sozusagen im Stillen, Jahr für Jahr, Job um Job, unterrichtet hier und dort und macht immer wieder und hauptsächlich freie Arbeiten – was ihm, wie ich vermute, am Liebsten ist. Er ist einfach gerne mit Künstler*Innen zusammen, in deren Aura, mit deren Werken und womöglich mit dem Geruch von Farbe (bei Richter, z.B.). Und das sieht man diesen Bildern einfach an, man spürt, dass sie wirklich gut sind, weiss aber nicht genau wieso, man kann das Geheimnis dieses Portraitisten nicht wirklich knacken. Will man das überhaupt? Ich war, als ich anfing Photographie kennenzulernen und zu lieben, zutiefst fasziniert von den Bildern von August Sander – meine damalige Freundin war Buchhandels-Lehrtochter und schenkte mir die wunderbare Schirmer-Ausgabe von *Menschen des 20. Jahrhunderts* – jedes Bild ein reiches Dokument und höchst spannend, Menschen aus einer anderen Epoche so nahe anzusehen, zu beobachten – und ich finde es keinesfalls vermessen, Albrecht Fuchs in die genau gleiche Tradition einzuordnen und hoffe natürlich, dass in fünfzig Jahren ein junger Mensch dieses Büchlein in die Hand nimmt und das gleiche Glück vom Menschsein und vom Wesen des Künstlerischen verspürt.   *—Dino Simonett, Donat, Springtime 2020*

Albrecht Fuchs Fifty-Three Portraits and a Haystack Conceived in Spring 2020 by Dino Simonett Graphic Design Dino Simonett with Martina Meier/Bureau Mia, Typeface Acumin Pro. Edition of One Thousand Books, printed at Druckerei Kettler, Bönen; bound at Buchbinderei Terbeck, Coesfeld. ISBN 978-3-906313-34-4 Simonett & Baer simonettbaer.com   **Cinque Bellini, per cortesia!*

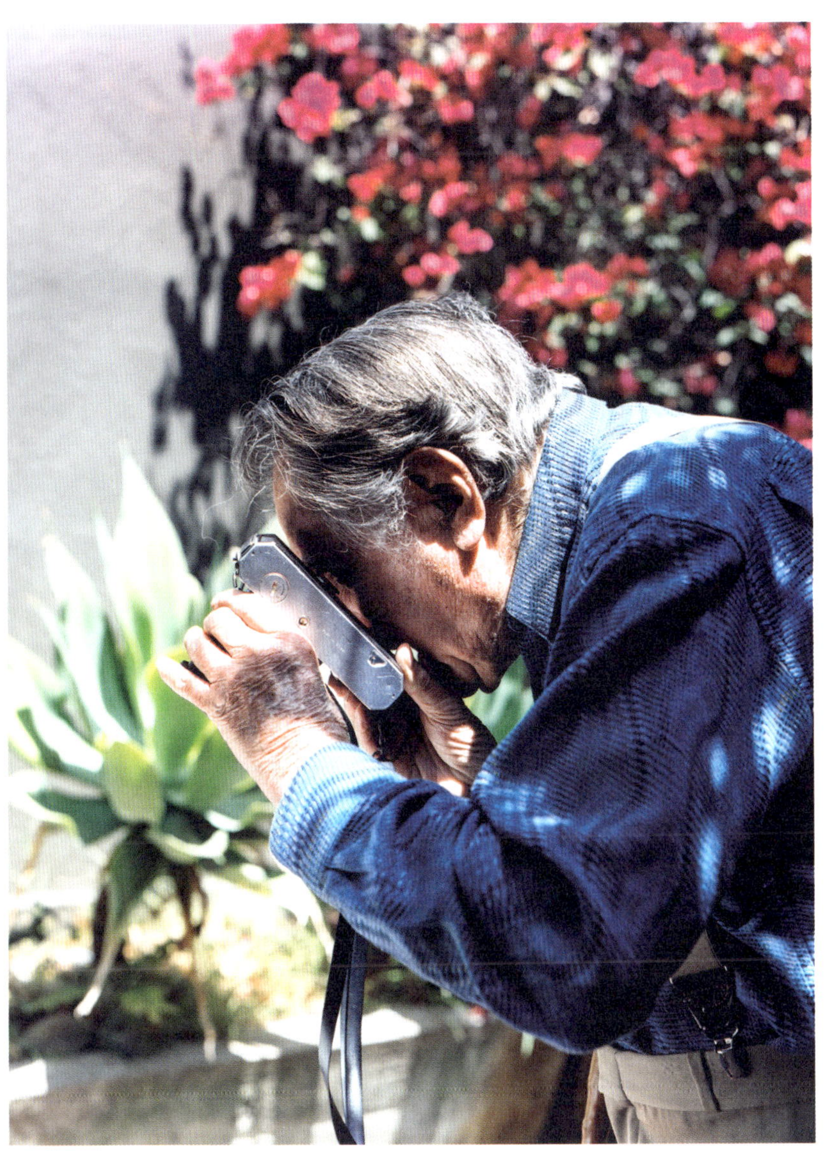

Julius Shulman, Photographer, Los Angeles 2004

Albrecht Fuchs Fifty-Three Portraits and a Haystack